"I've come to count on Paul Tripp's books being biblical, Christ-centered, deep, engaging, and well-written. *Sex and Money* is no exception. Its insights into our cultural idolatries and God's transforming grace are priceless."
    Randy Alcorn, author, *The Purity Principle* and *Managing God's Money*

"Fresh. Honest. Real. Paul Tripp tackles the familiar snares of sex and money with fresh perspective, honest answers from God's Word, and a real sense of our need for God's grace. I commend this new resource to you from my friend and ministry partner."
    James MacDonald, Senior Pastor, Harvest Bible Chapel; author, *Vertical Church*

"Sex and money. Are there any other subjects that occupy our thoughts more than these? Are there any other subjects that enslave our lives more than these? Paul Tripp provides insight into how we have turned these blessings from God into bondage and how a Godward perspective is the only way that they can be put back into their proper place in service to him. All who have struggled with these issues, which includes most everyone, will find practical, biblically grounded help in these pages."
    Tim Witmer, Professor of Practical Theology, Westminster Theological Seminary, Philadelphia; author, *The Shepherd Leader* and *The Shepherd Leader at Home*

"Paul Tripp reaches out to those weighed down by the sexual insanity and rampant materialism of our day. With careful biblical teaching, grace, and gospel at the heart of his argument, Tripp explains that it is only when we recognize God as the unchallenged master of our hearts that everything else will be in its rightful place. As he writes, 'The gospel is the only reliable diagnostic when it comes to sex and money, and because it provides the only reliable diagnostic, the gospel also graces us with the only truly effective cure.' This is a humble, hopeful, relevant book—a wonderful reminder that Jesus's way truly is easy and his burden light. I highly recommend it."
    Chris Brauns, Pastor, The Red Brick Church, Stillman Valley, Illinois; author, *Unpacking Forgiveness*

"I always benefit from Paul Tripp's relentless focus on how the posture and beliefs of our heart are the seat of our behavior. In *Sex and Money*, he has taken two of the greatest idols and unmasked them against the glorious gospel. If you really want to unseat the insanity and power of lust and materialism in your life, this book will take you to the one true solution—Jesus himself."
    Jay Thomas, Lead Pastor, Chapel Hill Bible Church; coauthor, *Sex, Dating, and Relationships*

SEX &
MONEY

SEX &
MONEY

PLEASURES THAT LEAVE YOU EMPTY
AND GRACE THAT SATISFIES

PAUL DAVID TRIPP

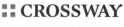 CROSSWAY

WHEATON, ILLINOIS

Hardcover ISBN: 978-1-4335-3649-6
PDF ISBN: 978-1-4335-3650-2
Mobipocket ISBN: 978-1-4335-3651-9
ePub ISBN: 978-1-4335-3652-6

Crossway is a publishing ministry of Good News Publishers.

LB		23	22	21	20	19	18	17	16	15	14	13
15	14	13	12	11	10	9	8	7	6	5	4	3	2	1

For new morning mercies and daily rescuing grace
I am eternally grateful.

CONTENTS

Preface   11

1   Sorry, but We've Gone Crazy   13

2   The Dangerous Dichotomy   27

3   So Why Do We Do the Things We Do?   41

4   The Highest Pleasure   55

5   Sex: The Big Picture   67

6   If Sex Is about Worship, Then It Can't Be Just about You   83

7   If Sex Is about Relationship, Then It Can't Be Just about You   99

8   If Sex Is about Obedience, Then It Can't Be Just about You   113

9   So Where Do We Go from Here?   127

10 Money Matters   143

11 Treasure Hunters   157

12 Money Is Not the Problem—Love Is   171

13 You Can't Take It with You   185

14 Are You Living Like You're Poor?   201

General Index   215

Scripture Index   219

PREFACE

It's the afternoon following the morning that I finished the book that you're now reading. The best description of my mood right now is that I am a sad celebrant. I am devastated at what this book has exposed in me. I am grieved by the lust that still resides in my heart, and I am saddened by the evidence that I still throw away money on things that simply don't matter. But I am far from hopeless, because writing this book has excited me at an even deeper level than ever before with the liberating and transforming power of the grace of the Lord Jesus.

I am sad to think that when it comes to sex and money we still buy into the legalism that says if we can organize people's lives, give them the right set of rules, and attach them to efficient systems of accountability, we can deliver people from their sex-and-money insanity. The fact that we can look at the power of sex-and-money sin to deceive and enslave people and feel comfortable in our reliance on the scant power of human intervention is itself insane. Few areas of the human struggle reveal more powerfully the sad sinfulness of sin than the sex-and-money evils that are done thousands of times every day.

Yet in the face of all of this, there is still robust reason for joy. All over, the church of Jesus Christ is returning once again to the hope of the gospel. All over, Christian leaders young and old are looking to the gospel of Jesus Christ to help them diagnose sex-and-money problems while at the same time holding out to those who are tempted, weak, or addicted the hope that is found only in the grace of Jesus.

Still, it is sad to think of how many people will look today to sex and money to give them what sex and money cannot give and, in so doing, give way to temptation and deepen their addiction. It is sad to think of how many people in their shame will deny the wrong of what they are doing and the depth of their enslavement. And while so many struggle in private, it is sad to see that the surrounding culture seems to get more and more sex-and-money insane with every passing day.

Yet in the face of all of this there is a happy rest in knowing that Jesus still reigns and will continue to advance the march of his kingdom until the last enemy is under his foot. He reigns over all the situations, locations, and relationships that would otherwise give you and me cause for despair. He reigns for his own glory and your good. And his reign is your guarantee that he will deliver all that he has promised you because only he can guarantee he'll make good on his promises in the places where he rules; by the way, that's everywhere.

So, go ahead and read this book as a sad celebrant. I hope that at times it will bring you to tears and at other times cause you to shout for joy. Rejoice with a frown or celebrate with tears. It really is what we should be doing between the "already" and the "not yet," while we still wait with the assurance that our Messiah will bring our sex-and-money struggles to an end.

Paul David Tripp
October 11, 2012

1

SORRY, BUT WE'VE GONE CRAZY

She's thirteen and the thing she can't stop thinking and talking about is her impending breast development. For her, being a woman is all about the size of one's breasts.

She's fifteen and is quite the self-appointed expert when it comes to oral sex. She doesn't just see herself as knowledgeable but as a bit experienced as well. What she likes about oral sex is that it's a way of having sex that "isn't really sex."

I've told my wife that during the summer months it's hard to walk down the street in Center City Philadelphia, where we live, and to know where to put your eyes, because there are so many women in various stages of undress.

Tim is seventeen, and in ways he doesn't recognize, he's already been trained to view women as objects whose value is attached to physical beauty and body shape.

George is married with three children; he seems to have a good marriage, but he masturbates at least once a day. His wife doesn't know it, but he's done it for years.

They came to me after a conference, carrying with them a combination of heart-brokenness and anger. They wanted to know what to do about their son who seemed hopelessly addicted to Internet pornography. I asked how old he was, thinking I would hear that he was in his teens or early twenties. To my shock, and speaking through his shame, the father said to me, "Eight." Eight! Let it sink in. Eight!

At a conference in South Africa they asked if they could have lunch with me. After the meal they told me their story. Their son, a newly married intern pastor, had been having sex with a college girl from the student ministry over which he was responsible.

In the big cities around the world you are considered a hopelessly old-fashioned bigot if you don't think same-sex marriage is not only a wonderful idea but also a civil right.

You can barely watch a video, look at a car ad, or hear a popular song without having your morals assaulted.

Sandra is twenty, and her definition of cool, fashionable clothes is those that are designed to reveal the body. Her clothes tend to be tight, short, and often low-cut. Sandra is a Christian who in many ways takes her faith seriously.

He asked to counsel with me because he knew he was in trouble. He was literally stalking women in the evenings after his seminary classes. He would hang around Starbucks and follow the most attractive women home, of course, never letting them know what he was doing.

How many teachers, how many coaches, have been arrested for having sex with the students that we've entrusted to their care?

There's a popular website that connects people who want to be unfaithful to others who are desirous of the same.

An inner-city high school opens up a daycare next to the school building because so many of its female students have children.

So many people are texting sexually explicit pictures from their cell phones that the word *sexting* becomes part of the modern vocabulary.

Internet pornography is the most powerful economic engine of the World Wide Web.

Before high school seniors ever have the experience of a real job, they are bombarded with preapproved credit cards, a graduation gift from the major banks.

The lavish lifestyles of the rich and famous eat up countless hours of TV and Internet content.

Many, many couples, with multiple credit cards and a catalog of loans, carry a dangerous weight of debt into marriage, seemingly unaware and unafraid.

Hundreds of thousands of people regularly live beyond their means and spend their adult life trying to keep their head above the deepening waters of debt.

Luxury car dealers make loans available to people who can't actually afford luxury cars so that people can pretend to be more wealthy and successful than they really are.

Hundreds of thousands of people, living in houses bigger than they need and more expensive than they can afford, dread the unstoppable reality of foreclosure.

A parent of a child in the local high school buys him a $50,000 SUV for his sixteenth birthday, and one has to wonder, where do they go up from there?

The personal debt load of the average committed Christian is itself a scandal.

A family secures a second mortgage on their house and puts the proceeds in their ATM account so that they have more spending money available.

Many, many people live in a situation where income chases life-style in an anxiety-producing dance with debt.

The majority of the money contributed to the average evangelical church is given by a small minority of its members, and many regular attenders give little or never give.

Many couples living in major cities drop off their children at day-care every day because they say it's literally impossible to live and pay your bills without both husband and wife working full-time.

Many older adults will have to work even though they're retired because they dipped into their retirement accounts to pay down debt that was the result of a lifestyle that their paycheck couldn't afford.

• • •

Sex and money—you don't have to look very far to see that we're in big trouble in both areas. The news is littered with daily sex and/or money scandals. The content of the tabloids is enough to alert us to the fact that something has gone terribly wrong. It's hard to listen to any cultural discussion of either area that isn't infected with either self-deception or distortion of reality. Neither sex nor money can deliver the promises that we think they're making, and each area is more dangerous than we tend to think. Both function today in the surrounding culture like spiritual solvents eating away at the very fabric of the human community. Both have the perverse power to master your heart and in so doing determine the direction of your life. Both give you the buzz that you're in control while, at the very same time becoming the master that progressively chains you to their control. Both offer you an inner sense of well-being while having no capacity whatsoever to satisfy your heart. Both seduce you with the prospect of contentment-producing plea- sure, but both leave you empty and craving more. Both hold out the possibility of finally being satisfied but instead cause you to envy whoever it is that has more and better than you do. Both sell you the lie that physical pleasure is the pathway to spiritual peace. Both are work of the Creator's hands but tend to promise you what only the Creator can deliver. Both are beauti- ful in themselves but have become distorted and dangerous by means of the fall.

With all of this swirling around us and inside us, the church of Jesus Christ has been strangely silent and reticent in both areas. We seem to approach both areas with a timidity, reserve, and embarrassment that does not make personal, cultural, or bib- lical sense. Pastors are often hesitant to teach and preach about money issues as if somehow this topic is outside the boundaries of what they've been called by God to do. And if they're cautious in talking about money, they're even more so when it comes to the topic of sex. Meanwhile, in both areas the world around us seems to never stop talking.

Christian parents don't seem to do a very good job in disci- pling their children in either area. How many parents teach their children about the street-level dangers of loving money, about how easy it is to incur crushing debt, what it looks like to live within one's means, and how your relationship to and use of money will always reveal the true condition of your heart? How many parents do more than have one creepy, quasi embarrassed talk about sex, with joy once it's over and a determination never to talk about it again? How many young people from Christian homes are struggling with questions, confusion, and temptation, but wouldn't think of seeking the help and wisdom of their embarrassed and silent parents? How many parents provide a long-term safe, gracious, and nonjudgmental place for their teens to talk about sex, knowing that the questions and temptations of a thirteen-year-old are different from those of a fifteen-year-old, which are different from those of an eighteen-year-old? Meanwhile, the obsessions and distortions of an addicted culture are powerfully brought to the eyes, ears, and hearts of even the most conservative Christians by pervasive and intrusive media that is almost impossible to escape.

Yet God in his great wisdom, for his glory and our good, has chosen for us to live in a world where money is an unavoidable issue and sex is a significant part of the human experience. The issues of sex and money are important and unavoidable because God chose them to be. And because sex and money are the creations of God's hand and exist under the control of his sovereignty, they should be approached by us with reverence and awe, not with embarrassment and timidity. Sex and money came from him, belong to him, and continue to exist through him; to him be the glory.

God has also chosen for us to live in a world where the lies, deceptions, distortions, and temptations of sex and money are many. The address where you live is not a divine mistake. Your exposure to the variegated difficulties of life in this fallen world, with all of its delusions and temptations, is not in the way of God's plan; it *is* his plan. He, right here, right now, has you exactly where he wants you to be. He knows exactly what you're facing. He isn't trying to cope with or cover up a grand divine mistake. He isn't wringing his hands in celestial anxiety. He has carefully and wisely chosen for you to live right where you live, knowing full well what you will face. All of this is done with divine knowledge and purpose. Again, all of these dynamics exist for his ultimate glory and your redemptive good.

So we can't act with regard to sex and money as if we're

powerless, or it will be impossible to prepare for what we will all inevitably face. We can't allow ourselves to think we're alone in the struggle. We can't allow ourselves to live like modern evangelical monastics, as if separation from the world is the key to true righteousness. And we can't be lulled or intimidated into silence in two crucial areas of the human existence where the Creator has powerfully and clearly spoken. And we mustn't forget the lie-exposing, freedom-granting truths of the gospel of Jesus Christ. It's vital that we remember that the grace of the Lord Jesus Christ doesn't just address your need for past forgiveness or your need for future hope, but it addresses everything you face in the place where God has positioned you right here, right now. It's this gospel that provides the only reliable diagnostic when it comes to sex and money, and because it provides the only reliable diagnostic, the gospel also graces us with the only truly effective cure. The gospel has the power to make us sex-and-money wise, to keep us sex-and-money protected and sex-and-money bold, no longer willing to be sidelined by timidity and fear. The gospel graces us with everything we need to celebrate and participate in both areas in a way that honors God and fully enjoys the good things he's given us to enjoy.

WHY THIS BOOK NOW?

People ask me all the time what I am working on or what I intend to write next. They always follow the first question with a second: "Why that now?" And they've surely been intrigued when I've told them that I am working on a book about sex and money. They've been interested in why I've chosen these two things from all the topics I could be addressing, and they ask what I see around me that motivates me to write about them now. As I've thought about this over the last several months, there are three words that have come to mind again and again, and they are my best answer to the question. The words are: *insanity, addiction,* and *glory.*

Insanity

No, not mine, but the culture's. I'm deeply persuaded that when it comes to sex and money, we've gone culturally insane. The level of functional delusion, of self-deception and self-destruction that accompanies the way we approach these areas is simply crazy. You don't have to look very far to see that we've gone sex-and-money insane. We're in debt up to our ears, but we never fail to spend more. We've put sex in a place it was never intended to be, but we seem to fail to see the danger. Our children are sexualized before they're properly educated. They're taught the joys of materialism before they can calculate enough to make sense of their pocket change. I sat in a nice restaurant and was forced to listen to graphic descriptions of sexual "love" that was supposed to be mealtime background music. I have to tear up countless unsolicited credit cards, sent to my unsuspecting children who were being encouraged to incur debt before they ever had a decent job, let alone anything you could call a career. You have few female pop singers who are able to resist the powerful demands around them to disrobe and do dance routines that are little more than well-orchestrated simulations of sex. We surely do a better job teaching our children how to spend than we do teaching them how to be content and thankful. We do a better job of teaching our children the things that money can help them to acquire than we do the importance of being a good steward of the resources that God provides.

Young girls today surely worry more about the beauty of their faces and the shape of their bodies than they do about the quality of their character. Our heroes tend to be people who are young, rich, and sexy rather than heroes in the classic sense of what that word connotes. Young women attached their identity to how thin their nose is, to how full their lips are, and to the size of their breasts. We evaluate one another with terms like *hot* and *hunk* (they sound more like descriptions of chocolate). Terms like *penis* and *vagina*, *tits* and *ass*, are in the accepted vocabulary of primetime TV. Pornography is not restricted to the bad neighbors and the dark hallways of rundown buildings. No, it exists on mainstream Internet sites that are a Google click away from anyone with a computer and the most basic computer literacy.

The size of personal, corporate, and governmental debt is itself a testament to a culture that, when it comes to money, has simply lost its mind. And in our denial we actually think that the way to get ourselves out of the mess we have spent our way into is by spending more. The personal credit card has altered our worldview of money. We now accept that it's sane to regularly spend money that we haven't yet acquired, as long as we can continue to pay the service fees on the card!

Look around. Listen carefully. Take time to evaluate and consider. Examine the true desires of your own heart. We're in trouble because, in two profoundly important places in life, what the human community tends to look at as normal isn't normal at all. It's a web of descending degrees of madness. And in the midst of the madness there's only one window through which we can look at the worlds of sex and money and see with candor, clarity, and wisdom. This window is the gospel of the Lord Jesus Christ. And there is only one thing that can free us from the insanity that somehow, someway seems at some point to grip us all. It's the grace of that very same gospel. You see, the humbling truth is that when it comes to sex and money we don't have a thing problem; the things (sex and money) are not evil in themselves. We don't have an environment problem, as if our surroundings cause the difficulty. No, we are the problem. The counterintuitive reality is that it's only ever the evil inside us that magnetizes us toward and connects us to the evil that's outside of us. Since we are the problem, we really have a problem. We can run from a thing, we can change a relationship, we can move to a different location, but we can't escape ourselves. No, we need rescue, and because we need rescue, we need a rescuer who is wise, powerful, willing, and faithful. That rescuer is the Lord Jesus Christ. He is willing, he is wise, he is able, and he will not forsake us in our time of need.

Addiction

But there's a second word that motivated the writing of this book, *addiction*. The dynamic of addiction is that if you look to something that God created, to give you what it wasn't intended to give you, either you get discouraged quickly, and wisely abandon those hopes, or you go back again and again, and in so doing, you begin to travel down addiction's road. That created thing will give you a short-term buzz of euphoria, it will offer you temporary pleasure, it will provide a momentary sense of well-being, it will briefly make you feel that you're something, and it may even make your problems seem not so bad for a bit. It's all very intoxicating. It all feels great. The problem is that the created thing that you're looking to has no capacity to satisfy your heart. It wasn't designed to do that. It cannot give you inner peace. It cannot give you the heart rest of contentment. It cannot quiet your cravings. In a word, it cannot be your savior. And if you look outside of the Savior for something to be your savior, that thing will end up not being your savior but your master.

You'll love the short-term buzz, but you'll hate how short it is. So you'll have to go back again quickly to get another shot, and before long you've spent way too much time, energy, and money on something that can't satisfy; but because of what it has briefly done for you each time, you're convinced that you can't live without it. You're hooked and you may not know it. The thing you once *desired*, you're now persuaded that you *need*, and once you've named it a need, it has you.

Sex is powerfully pleasurable, but it cannot satisfy your heart. A shot of unexpected cash in your ATM account will make you smile, but it can't give you true happiness. The touch of another person will stimulate your body and your heart, but it will never leave you fulfilled. Money has the power to change something in your life, but it has no ability whatsoever to make you a better person.

You see, whether we know it or not, every human being lives in search of a savior. We are all propelled by a quest for identity, inner peace, and some kind of meaning and purpose. And we'll all look for it somewhere. Here's the bottom line: looking to creation to get what only the Creator can give you will always result in addiction of some kind. The thing that you hoped would serve you pulls you into its service. What seemed like freedom ends up being bondage. The thing is not the problem; what you've asked of it is.

Glory

This leads to a third word that lies at the foundation of what this book is about. That word is *glory*. As I have written before, human beings are hardwired for glory. That's why we're so attracted to glorious things. We love the glory of a great painting or a beautiful piece of music. We love the excitement of an athletic contest or a feat of daring. We love the sleight of hand of a great magician or the sizzle of a well-seared steak. We love the glory of a moment of success or the recognition of the people around us. We're attracted to the glory of wealth or the beauty of the human body. We're very powerfully oriented to glory, and because we are, we live in pursuit of it.

Animals are not like this. Rhinos don't celebrate the size of their horns. Deer don't gather for the bi-annual long-jump contest. Birds don't envy one another's feathers. Animals don't have this glory orientation, because they weren't made for God in the way that we are. Human beings are hardwired for glory because they were hardwired for God. The glory orientation that's inside of every person is meant to drive us to God.

Here's the problem. When God created the world, he dyed it with his glory. The created world really is glorious because God made it that way. But the created world is not in possession of *ultimate glory*, the kind of glory that can satisfy your heart. The glory of the created world is *sign* glory. All the glory of the created world is meant to be a sign that points us to the only glory that will ever give rest and peace to our hearts, the glory of God. We were designed to live for that glory. But we lose sight of the fact that the sign isn't the thing; it is there to point us to the thing, and in forgetting this, we ask the sign to do for us what it cannot do.

In this way, life this side of eternity really is one big, unceasing glory battle. There could be no bigger issue than this, than what glory will rule your heart, and in ruling your heart, control your thoughts, desires, choices, words, and behavior. Sinful human beings in functionally denying the existence of God will stop at the sign, won't care about what the sign points them to, and will ask of the sign what it will never be able to give. And that created thing with all its glory will not be their savior; no it will prove to be a cruel and inglorious master that takes much, but gives very little of what they were really seeking. Sex and money are glorious, but they were created to be fingers that point you to the one glory you were designed to live for, the glory of God.

IT'S ALL VERTICAL

If you've paid attention to our discussion so far, what I'm going to say next shouldn't surprise you. The words *insanity, addiction,* and *glory* point us to the fact that our problems with sex and money will never be solved horizontally. Sex and money madness are not first problems of situation, location, or relationship. Sex problems are not first biology or physiology problems. Societal sex addiction doesn't exist because the body is a problem. The fact that we are sexual beings is not the problem. Sex problems are not first the problem of modern media. Our money insanity is not the fault of money. This madness is not first a matter of budget. Our problem is not that credit exists or that things cost something. Our money madness isn't about situation, location, or relationship. Our problem in both of these areas isn't physical and horizontal. It's a matter of the heart. Our problems are deeply spiritual.

The apostle Paul says something very striking in 2 Corinthians 5:20. He says that God has called us to be ambassadors of one message. 24/7 we mustn't forsake the diagnosis and cure of this solitary message. This message echoes God's unceasing appeal. Here it is: "Be reconciled to God." You see, it's all vertical. The madness that we've briefly considered and that this book will unpack isn't first horizontal, so it won't be fixed horizontally. This insanity is vertical. It's only when God is in his rightful place as the unchallenged Master of our hearts that everything else in our lives will be in their appropriate place as well. When something else replaces him, insanity and chaos of some kind always result.

In ways that are formative and practical, we begin to serve the creation as we were designed to serve the Creator, no matter what we say we believe. But it never works; it only leaves us empty, driven, and dissatisfied, the victims of our own bad choices. What we hoped would help us has in fact hooked us. And we cannot run from our problem, because the problem is us. It's only when we live practically inside of what it means to be reconciled to God that we will hold the powerful glories of the created world in the way that they were designed to be held.

So take this journey with me. Either you have sex and money problems yourself, or you are near to someone who does. You've bought into the insanity, or someone near to you is mad. Look with me at these two places of cultural madness through the perfect window of the gospel of Jesus Christ and experience with me the wisdom and freedom that can be found only there.

2

THE DANGEROUS DICHOTOMY

Words are important. They give shape and meaning to things. Much of what you think, desire, know, and choose has been shaped by words. Words have been given special importance to human beings if for no other reason than the fact that God chose to reveal himself in words. We know God for his works (general revelation), but we primarily and specifically know him because of his words (special revelation). If you are a believer, the entire way that you think about yourself, life, and the world around you has been shaped by the words of God found on the pages of your Bible. In all things, your calling is to live inside the boundaries of what God has said. But here's where you just start. You must begin by understanding the importance, the life-shaping significance of the first four words of the Bible. You could argue that there are no more important words than these, that everything else the Bible says is built on the foundation of the thunderous implication of these four words. You can't understand yourself, you can't understand life, and you surely can't have a balanced view of the worlds of sex and money without understanding the worldview of these four words.

Your Bible begins with these four words: "In the beginning God," and with those four words everything in life is given its shape, purpose, and meaning. But for the purpose of our topics, these words do something very important. They destroy the validity of dividing life into things that are spiritual and things that are secular. This division has opened doors of danger to us as we think about sex and money. It's allowed us to live with a distance and dissonance between our worlds of sex and money and the principles and promises of Scripture. It's caused us to fail to look at these inescapable areas of human life from the vantage point of the gospel of Jesus Christ. It's caused us to not value the practical wisdom of Scripture and to shop for help elsewhere. It's caused us to not avail ourselves of the rescue that can be found only in the person and work of the Lord Jesus Christ. And it's allowed us to minimize the degree to which our use of money and our every sexual act are deeply and inescapably spiritual. The way you use money and the manner in which you participate in sex always reveal the true spirituality of your heart.

So I want to take time to unpack the implications of those four words in Genesis 1:1 and apply them to the worlds of sex and money. Here's the summary of the implications to follow. *A gospel-centered approach to sex and money that avoids the insanity of the surrounding culture must begin with looking at life through the window of the doctrine of creation.* The four words that kick off the biblical story of creation, "In the beginning God," drive us to the following six implications.

1) God exists and is the center of all things.

It is humble and significant to realize that the biblical story doesn't begin with us. It begins with God. It's important to recognize that the story that unfolds on the pages of your Bible is God's story. He stands on center stage. He has the most important lines. The following spotlight is always on him. The story moves according to his will and by his plan. It's all for him, from him, through him, and about him. He zealously holds on to his position at the center of all things. He will not forsake his position of authority or give his control to another. He is the center, the important one, and the Lord of glory. Your understanding of everything in your life must begin here.

Your life is not about you; it is about him. It's vital to know that you were born into a universe that by its very nature is a celebration of him. It's only when he is in his proper place in your heart, that is, at the center, that everything else will be in its appropriate place and balance of your life. What this means practically is that everything exists for his pleasure and glory and not for yours. So you and I must approach everything in a way that gives God the glory that belongs to him. If you forget him and his glory, you'll use things for no higher purpose than your own glory, and in so doing you'll misuse them in some way. Again, the recognition of God's centrality in all that is, and the existence of all things for his glory, is not so much about being super-spiritual. This is about recapturing the full meaning of your humanity. This is the way all human beings were made to live. To insert yourself into the center of your world is to violate the very nature of the world, and that isn't the fundamental way that all things were designed to operate. To violate basic creation order and design never goes anywhere good, no matter what dimension of our lives we're talking about.

Practical, everyday "me-ism," where the world is reduced to the small confines of your comfort, your pleasure, your control, your happiness, and your ease never works. It doesn't work because it runs cross-grain against the way you and the world you live in were meant to operate. You see, it's simply not about you, and when you make it about you nothing good results. God-forgetting self-sovereignty is dangerous to you and destructive to your heart and will cause you to use things in a way they were not intended to be used. Because of this, "me-ism" never results in long-term peace, rest, satisfaction, and joy.

When you put yourself and your particular definition of pleasure at the center of your world, you're not only rejecting God's wisdom and rebelling against his authority, but you're also questing for his position. But God, in his zeal for his own glory and for your good, won't exit his position and give it to you.

You just can't properly understand and participate in the worlds of sex and money without this perspective. Think about this. Our problems with sex don't begin with lust, with bad choices, or with sexual misbehavior. Our problems with sex begin when we forget that God must be at the center of this part of our lives as he must be with any other. When you've no greater motivation in sex than your own satisfaction, you are already in sexual trouble even if you don't know it yet. *How have you tended to put yourself in the center of your world of sexuality?*

When you've no higher purpose for your money than to spend what you get on your pleasure, your world of money is already in trouble even though you may not see signs of trouble yet. Our problems with money don't begin when we spend more than we make; they begin when we forget that God must be at the center of this part of our lives. When you have no bigger purpose for your cash than your own enjoyment, you're already in money trouble even though the signs of trouble may not be jumping out at you yet. *Have you tended to have a God-forgetting, utilitarian view of money, viewing it only as a means of getting stuff or for paying bills?*

Whether or not you functionally recognize it, at the epicenter of your worlds of sex and money exists a God of awesome power, glory, and grace. Sex and money in their rightful place in your heart and life always begin by recognizing that he is at the center.

2) God is the creator and owner of all that exists.

My words here, "God is the creator and owner of all that exists," have been chosen carefully. You cannot have the first word (creator) without the other (owner). The concept of creation always carries with it the resulting concepts of design and ownership. Perhaps two of the most important questions you could ask about anything in your life are, What was the purpose of the Creator for this thing when it was made? and What does it look like for me to recognize the Creator's ownership over this thing as I use it in my daily living? Because you and I are creatures and not the creator, it isn't our prerogative to relate to our lives and the things in our lives as if we are the owners and designers. When you act as though everything in your wallet belongs to you, you have an ownership posture toward money. When you act like it's your right to use the money you've earned according to your purpose, you have a designer's posture toward money.

Here's what's important to understand: human beings were designed to be resident managers of the created world that God owns. God makes and owns the beautiful garden of Eden, places Adam and Eve in it, and then commissions them to live in and care for the garden he made and owns. They don't own what they've been given. They don't make the rules for what's been made. They don't get a vote when it comes to the purpose for their own lives and for everything else that's been made. They're there to recognize God's ownership by fulfilling his purpose.

Now I find these perspectives to be very convicting. When I'm about to buy whatever it is that I want at the moment but that I don't actually need, is there any consciousness in me that my money belongs to the Lord? When I'm thinking about physical intimacy with Luella, is there any consciousness in me at that moment that my body and my sexuality belong to the Lord? Let's be honest—it's counterintuitive to think this way. What's natural is to get out my wallet and get what I want and forget that God even exists. It's natural to be propelled by sexual desire, forgetting that there is One who owns every aspect of our sexuality.

I'm afraid that we don't think in helpful ways in these areas because we've reduced our relationship with sex and money to a set of rules. But God's rules aren't arbitrary. They're not just a set of disconnected moral abstractions. They don't make any sense when viewed or presented that way. God's rules are rooted in relationship. It is here alone that they get their rationality and beauty. You see, we were designed for relationship with God, a relationship in which we would daily recognize his position as our creator and our position as his creatures. All of God's rules are an outgrowth, an expression of, or an application of the thing for which we were made—relationship with him. This relationship was to be shaped by worshipful love and joyful obedience. Celebrating God's existence, wisdom, power, and glory would mean that we would have no complaint with staying inside his boundaries.

What this means is that you cannot have a sensible discussion of sexual dysfunction of human culture by just discussing the evidences of its sexual insanity. You can recognize and critique dysfunction only when you're examining it from the perspective of ownership, purpose, and design. You cannot have a rational discussion of money troubles by starting with a few principles of how to use your money, because those principles, as wise as they are, only make sense in the face of the reality that there was a purpose for all that's been made that resided in the mind of the Creator. To know God's mind is to know his purpose, and to know his purpose is to understand how money is meant to be used, and to know how money is meant to be used allows you to then recognize and critique its misuse.

There is one other thing that needs to be said here. It's important to understand that *ownership* living, where you live as if your life and everything in it belongs to you, never results in the lasting rest, joy, peace, happiness, and fulfillment that every human being seeks. We need only the shocking and sad story of the disobedience in the garden to tell us where ownership living leads. You cannot have the peace of heart that's the quest of everyone and violate the core principle of the universe, that is, the centrality of God in all things.

3) Because God is a spirit and we are made in his image
and for relationship with him, all of life is spiritual.

Human beings tend to make sense out of life by dividing it up
into meaningful categories. Political, work, economic, education,
gender, social, familial, age, and entertainment categories function
as a conceptual toolkit for us. You hear the category, and you know
in some general way what you're dealing with. This is all well
and good as long as your order-giving categories are good ones.
Bad categories can lead to sloppy, nonsensical thinking but more
importantly to bad living. I'm afraid that this is what's happened
with the age-old categories of *spiritual* and *secular*. You cannot take
the first four words of the Bible seriously and be comfortable
with dividing your world into the secular and the spiritual. Now,
I know that there are endeavors in life that are self-consciously
religious, and there are activities that are decidedly not. But that
isn't what we're talking about here. We're talking about dividing
your life into things that have to do with God and things that don't
or, even more dangerously, things in life that belong to God and
things that belong to you. So God gets the religious, devotional,
churchistic part of your existence, and everything else is secular,
that is, not necessarily connected to the spiritual part of your life,
as long as in those areas you are keeping the Ten Commandments.

The first four words of the Bible immediately alert you to the
fact that you cannot divide up life this way. It cannot be sectored
into the spiritual and secular: God and mine, religious and non-
religious, faith and facts, or whatever other categories you would
use to separate things that are Godward and things that are not.
You end up with a dangerous schizophrenia of heart that creates havoc at the street level. Since all of life was made by God, it
exists through him, is there for him, and is designed to operate
according to his plan. There is no purely secular domain of your
life. Your very existence as a human being made in God's image
connects you to him all the time. Everywhere you go and in everything you do, you encounter things that were made by him,

connecting you to him once again. He reveals himself in powerful ways in the creation he has made. God is inescapable. He is literally the environment in which you live. As I have said many, many times, you can't get up in the morning without bumping into God.

So sex is not an a-religious thing. Sex is deeply spiritual. Your relationship to your own sexuality and the sexuality of others will always reveal your heart. Your sexual life will always be an expression of what you truly worship. Sex is deeply religious. In sex either you are self-consciously submitting to God, or you are setting yourself up as God. Sex is not just a human relationship thing. It's never simply a horizontal thing. Sex is always connecting you to the God who created your body, who gave you eyes to see and a heart that desires, and who tells you how you are to steward this aspect of your personhood.

Money is not a secular thing. It is much more than how much currency you have in your wallet and in your bank account. It is much, much more than hitting the buy button on your iPhone. Your thoughts about money and your use of money always are an expression of the deepest treasures of your heart. Money will expose what you really value and what you truly serve. Money will be a means that you use to insert yourself into the middle of your world, or it will be an expression of your constant awareness that you were put on earth to serve another. The big question of money is never, "Can I afford it?" No, it is always "How can I invest what I've been given in a way that gives honor to the One who has entrusted it to me?"

Your money world is a spiritual world. It's a world shaped by the worship of God or by some kind of idolatry. There is simply no escaping God in your world of money.

4) Since God is the creator and controller of all things, he alone is worthy of our worship.

I've said it already, but I want to expand on what it means here. Your worlds of sex and money are worlds of worship. Now

I'm sure for many readers this needs explanation. For many of us, *worship* is a tricky word. We tend to think of worship in restricted, formal worship ways. But what's important to understand is that worship is your identity as a human being. You were designed for worship. This means that you're always attaching the hopes, dreams, peace, motivations, joy, and security of your heart to something. So you don't just worship on Sunday; you worship your way through every day of your life. A worshiper is who you are; worship is what you do. So sex is an act of worship in some way. Your use of money is an act of worship in some way. When you think of worship, don't just think of a weekend religious activity; think of a lifestyle. Let me explain further.

There are four aspects to the lifestyle of worship that are laid out in Scripture. First, to worship means to *bow down*. This is the devotional, affective part of worship. The posture connoted by these words is important. In bowing down, I kneel before God and offer him the affections of my heart. I give him the honor that is his due. I bring to him the deepest of offerings, the love of my heart. I am bowing to his majesty, his authority, his centrality, and his holiness. I am recognizing that he exists and that I was made by and for him. Remember, as you use sex and money, you're always bowing down to someone or something. You cannot escape the "bowing down" aspect of these significant areas of your life.

Second, to worship means to *obey*. Here I recognize God's wisdom and his rule. In obedience I am stating that I know that my life doesn't belong to me, that I wasn't created to write my own rules. Obedience is worship at the most mundane of levels. Here I'm submitting the detailed choices and actions of my life to God's greater wisdom and his greater authority. So in sex you are either worshiping God by willingly submitting to his wise and good rules or writing your own rules, and in so doing, telling yourself that you're smarter than God. In money you are willingly staying inside God's money boundaries, acknowledging the fact that he is wise and in control, or you're stepping over God's boundaries because you think your life belongs to you and you're capable of writing your own rules.

Also, to worship means to *trust*. To trust means to willingly place your life, your welfare, your future, and your inner sense of well-being in God hands. It's not only to assent to the fact that he is good and his way is always right but also to think, desire, speak and act as if you really do. Your sexual activity always expresses trust in someone or something. Your use of money always pictures trust in someone or something.

Finally, to worship means to *serve*. Here I submit the agenda, the hopes and dreams, or the plan of my life to the greater plans of God. In worship I walk away from my little self-satisfied kingdom of one where I reign as a self-appointed sovereign, and I give the time, energy, and resources of my life to the plans, purposes, and work of the kingdom of God. It's inescapably true that you always have sex in service of one of these two kingdoms, and the same is true of your use of money. In sex and money you will remember that God didn't give you his grace to make your little kingdom successful but to welcome you to a much bigger and much better kingdom.

Your world of sex and money is a world of worship. The big question is not "Are you out of trouble and out of debt?" but "In sex and money, what in the world is it that you are worshiping?"

5) When it comes to sex and money, we've been infected with the world's insanity because we've bought into a false and dangerous dichotomy.

I'm afraid that there's more of this *spiritual versus secular* dichotomy hanging around in our thinking and the way we approach life than we may think. And when we've divided our world this way, we've little defense against the insanity of the surrounding culture. Let me give you a very practical example.

Think of the way that most Christian parents talk to their children about these two topics. When it comes to sex, they tend first to have one quasi-embarrassed talk about how the bodies of men and women are made and how they sexually function. Then they give their soon-to-be-sexually alive and interested young person a set of dos and don'ts. Now, this talk simply doesn't prepare young people to defend themselves against the constant stream of sexual insanity that they'll be exposed to almost everywhere they look.

These parents mean well, but they've not rooted the whole topic of sexuality in the reality of the existence of God, in the glory of his love, wisdom, power, and grace; and the peace, fulfillment, and security of living the way we were design to live—for him. Armed with little more than an I'm-not-supposed-to approach to sexuality, they have little protection from the seductive voices that will constantly whisper in their ears.

Think of how Christian parents talk to their children about money. They want their children to learn how to budget, to learn how to use a bank account, and to know the danger of debt. These topics are all well and good, but they won't protect your children against the money insanity that's everywhere around them. The child doesn't know his own worship nature and how money always expresses worship. The child doesn't know that he was made for God, that money is to be used not only for his pleasure but also for God's. He doesn't know that money security isn't found first in a good budget but in seeking God's kingdom. He doesn't know that when your heart loves what God says to love, your wallet will tend to be in good shape. And because he hasn't had money discussed in the context of these rich truths, he's unprepared for the money idolatry that he'll be constantly bombarded with.

It's only an everything-is-spiritual-because-everything-is-worship view of life that builds for us a defense against the insanity that's both inside and outside of us.

6) The purpose of the cross is to reconcile us to God
and restore God to his rightful place in our hearts.

The first four words of the Bible explain to us the rest of the story of the Bible. It's only in the face of the reality that we were made for God and that everything exists for him that the necessity of Jesus's coming and the cross make sense. Since sin separates us from God and causes us to live for ourselves, and since there's nothing we can do to earn our way back into God's favor, a savior had to come. The Savior would have to live the life that we should have lived and die the death that was our due and rise again, defeating sin and death. All of this was necessary so that we would not only be guaranteed eternal life but also be reconciled to God.

You see, it's only when we're in right relationship with God, when we're living for him and not for ourselves, when we're entrusting ourselves to his good purpose and following his wise rule, that everything in our lives will be in its proper place. Hope for sex-and-money sanity is found only in one place: at the foot of the cross of the Lord Jesus Christ. Sanity in these two important areas will never be found in trying harder and doing better, because what you need most to defend yourself against doesn't live outside of you but inside of you. The greatest of sex-and-money dangers you carry around inside of you, and you take them with you wherever you go and to whomever you're with.

So the first four words of the Bible, "In the beginning God," drive me to one conclusion: I need a Savior of glorious and transforming grace, because I need to be saved from me. Without the grace of this Savior, I'll join the company of the insane and use my body and my resources in ways they were never meant to be used. But there's hope for me, because this Savior has come, and he's poured out his grace. He gives me much more than a set of rules; he gives me himself. Not only does he forgive me, but he comes and lives inside of me, and in so doing, begins to transform me at the causal core of my personhood, my heart. By grace he daily fights on my behalf. By grace he causes me to love wisdom and to hate foolishness. By grace he leads me to love his kingdom more than I love my own. By grace he convicts me when I'm wrong and restores me with his forgiveness. By grace he welcomes me to run to him and not from him when I've failed to measure up. And someday by grace he'll take me to a place where the insanity is no more.

If all of life is spiritual, then the deepest sex-and-money need of every human being who's ever taken a breath is his need of a Savior. He has come! There is hope!

3

SO WHY DO WE DO
THE THINGS WE DO?

He was in trouble long before he knew it. As he assessed his life, he concluded that he was okay, but he wasn't. He saw himself as a mature Christian, a committed family man and a diligent worker. But he was running toward disaster without any sense of concern or fear.

He had worked with her for years. They were on a management team and were often in meetings together. For almost a decade their relationship had been strictly business, that is, until that day when she asked if she could share a table with him in the executive dining room. That morning had been ridiculously stressful. His children were out of control, and he and his wife were not in a very good place. By the time he left for work, everybody was mad at everybody, and his good-bye gesture to his wife was a dirty look rather than the usual perfunctory kiss.

He must have had the posture and facial expression of a beaten man, because when she sat down with her lunch tray, her opening line was not about business; it was about him. "You look like you've been hit by a Mac truck," she said, half jokingly.

"You have no idea," he responded.

"Oh, yeah?" she replied.

"It's not work," he said. "Things are great here; it's home. Sometimes it all just seems impossible. Too many complicated relationships with too many people all at once. It's all I can do to turn off the stress before I get here so I can concentrate on the job and not get myself fired," he moaned.

"If you're anything at home like you are here, you must be a pretty good husband and father. I'm sure your family is blessed to have you around," she said as she looked at her watch, excused herself, and rushed out of the room.

He watched her leave, thinking, "That was really nice; the most encouragement I've gotten in months." He went back to work and his busy life and didn't think about her for days until they had their first semi-monthly executive meeting. He noticed her in ways that he hadn't noticed her before. She got his attention in ways that the other participants hadn't. He tried not to look at her because he didn't want to make her uncomfortable, but he kept looking at her. After the meeting he went back to his overloaded desk. He tried to deny it, but a couple days later he was glad that she came into his office to ask him a few departmental questions. Before she left she asked, "Are things less stressful at home?" He smiled and rolled his eyes as she exited his office. He sat, watching her go, completely unaware that something dramatic and important, potentially life-changing, was happening in his heart. He still thought he was okay.

In the kind of denial that seems to accompany these temptations, he told himself that nothing had changed, but it had. He began to come to work hoping that he would see her. No, he didn't want a relationship with her, and no, he'd entertained no thoughts whatsoever of sex with her, but in his heart his relationship to her had definitely changed. He didn't often eat in the lunchroom, but he began to regularly. He told himself that it was good for the department, but that's not why he was there. He was there in the hopes that she would be there. She often was, and the occasion of their having lunch together happened more frequently.

With each lunch something was happening in his heart that

he seemed completely unaware of. His affection compass was increasingly pointing in her direction. He hadn't abandoned his commitment to his wife, and he surely hadn't entertained any thoughts of leaving his marriage, but his heart had moved, and because it had, it wouldn't be long before his body would move as well. He told himself that she was just another colleague, but she wasn't. He told himself that it was important to develop solid friendships with fellow workers, but he seemed to have that bond only with her. Their conversations became more frequent, more planned, and more personal, but he still had no sense of danger.

In one of their times in the hallway, they were laughing about something, and she touched his hand. He felt a buzz at that moment that he had only ever felt with his wife. She had touched him and he liked it. He wanted her to touch him again. No, he wasn't think of sex, but he liked her, and he liked being close to her. He liked the thought of being physically close. The heart that he should have protected long before was now no longer searching or attracted; it was hooked. But he simply didn't recognize how hooked he was.

His wife began to be concerned. It wasn't because he was staying late at work; he wasn't. It wasn't that she had found an unexplained receipt or something on his cell phone. No, she noticed differences in the way he related to her. He seemed distant and even less communicative. He was surely more impatient and irritable than usual. He had quit giving her that perfunctory kiss. And it had been a long time since he had shown any interest in sex with her. She had approached him several times with her concern, and he had told her that it must be the burdens from work that he carried home, and he would try to do better at leaving them at the door. But nothing changed. She was worried, but she didn't know what to worry about.

Meanwhile his relationship with the woman at work had gotten quite physical. I don't mean *physical* in an overtly sexual sense. What I mean is that their relationship had become quite tactile. He would put his arm around her when he asked how she was doing. She would stand with her body actually touching him when they were waiting in the hallway for a meeting. He would grab her hand when he was making a point or touch her shoe with his shoe under the table in a meeting. All of this appeared to him and maybe to others as harmless, but it wasn't harmless at all. It wasn't harmless because all of it was sexual, highly sexual. He had weeks earlier committed adultery in his heart; that is, he had shifted the affection of his heart from his wife to his fellow worker, and now he was beginning to commit adultery with his body. It was all office-acceptable foreplay, and it wouldn't be long before sex would follow.

It was in the stairwell of the parking garage as they were both leaving for the day that she reached up and gave him a kiss on the cheek as she said good-bye. He looked around to see if anyone was near and responded with a kiss on the lips. Embarrassed, they both rushed away, but it wouldn't be long before they rented a hotel room for the disaster that they'd been heading toward for a very long time.

He sat with me, now estranged from his wife and having left his well-paying job depressed, self-righteous, and confused. "She knew I was married, and she set me up anyway," he said defensively. It was the same old self-righteous, self-atoning delusion I'd heard many times before. He'd thrown away a wonderful marriage to a good lady and his relationship to three beautiful children for twenty minutes of sexual pleasure. He knew that what he'd done was wrong, but he still held on to the possibility that he wasn't to blame. Adulterous, yet innocent—how does that happen?

SO WHY DO WE DO THE THINGS WE DO?

It was a dramatic game-changing moment. It's recorded for us in Matthew 5:27–30. Jesus is unfolding the gospel principles of his kingdom. I've often wondered what the reaction of the crowd was as he spoke these words:

> You have heard that it was said, "You shall not commit adultery." But I say to you that everyone who looks at a woman with lustful intent has already committed adultery with her in his heart. If your right eye causes you to sin, tear it out and throw it away. For it is better that you lose one of your members than that your whole body be thrown into hell. And if your right hand causes you to sin, cut it off and throw it away. For it is better that you lose one of your members than that your whole body go into hell.

In these words not only does Christ lay out the original intent of God's law and defines where the real moral battle is raging, but he also drops a bomb on any hope that legalism can produce righteous living. Let me give you the helicopter view of this little passage and then draw out some of its implications for our topic.

These words are humbling to hear but vitally important to consider because Christ is saying something to us that is counterintuitive to the way most of us think about ourselves and try to make sense out of our lives. From 50,000 feet, what Christ is doing here in the area of sex is answering the question that every human being asks at some time: "Why do people do the things they do?" Why do we say the things we say and make the decisions we make? Why do we successfully fight some things and willingly give in to others? Why do we tell ourselves that we won't do certain things but end up doing them anyway? Why?

The wars of sex and money are never just a battle with the temptations of the surrounding culture; they're never just about behavior or about what we do with our bodies. Christ is saying that our behavior is more directed by what's inside us than the people and situations outside us. He's saying that sexual struggles are inescapably struggles of the heart. Physical adultery is simply the body going where the heart has long ago gone. And as he says this, Christ gives thoughts and desires the moral value of actions.

You don't cross the adultery boundary when you have illicit sex. You cross the boundary when you give your heart to thoughts and desires that are outside of God's will for you. You will never win the battle with sexual sin by just attempting to harness your behavior, because every wrong sexual act is connected to a decision, which is connected to a desire in your heart. You always give your heart away before you surrender your body to what is wrong.

I want also to say here that although this discussion focuses on sex, all that we say about sexual sin and temptation can be said of our misuse of money. Money problems are always heart problems. When in Matthew 6:19 Jesus uses the word "treasure," he locates the struggles of money and materialism in the heart. A treasure is more than a physical thing. The physical treasures that we pile up always reveal the true values of our hearts. The treasures that we hoard always picture the riches that our hearts crave. What is a treasure? It's something that has risen in value or importance in our heart and is now in some kind of control of what we think and what we desire. So money craziness is about something more than the influence of the people and the culture that surrounds us. Our misuse of money is the result of the misplaced treasures of our heart.

Listen to the hard-to-hear words of Mark 7:20–23:

And he said, "What comes out of a person is what defiles him. For from within, out of the heart of man, come evil thoughts, sexual immorality, theft, murder, adultery, coveting, wickedness, deceit, sensuality, envy, slander, pride, foolishness. All these evil things come from within, and they defile a person."

Notice that Jesus doesn't say, "Hey guys, it's very simple. The problem is, you live in this broken and evil world that isn't functioning as I intended. It's populated with sinful people who will seduce you into doing what's wrong. So if you want to live a godly life, you have to determine to separate yourself from both." But that's how we tend to think. I've heard adulterous husbands say to me, "Paul, if you lived with my wife, you would understand why I did what I did." I've heard adulterous women blame the seductive power of the man. I've heard parents of a pregnant teenager blame TV, YouTube, and Facebook. I've heard pastors who've committed sexual sin point to the lonely burdens of stressful ministry. What I hear again and again is people instinctively pointing outside of themselves to answer the question "Why did I do what I did?" But listen to the words of Jesus and let them sink in. "What comes out of a person is what defiles him."

Here's where the words of Christ drive us: our struggle with sexual sin is not first a struggle with the environment in which we live or with the people that we live near. Our struggle with sexual sin reveals the dark and needy condition of our hearts. We are our biggest problem. When it comes to sexual sin, the greatest sexual danger to any human being anywhere lives inside of him and not outside of him. Isolation, changes of location and relationship, and the management of behavior never work because they don't target the place where the problem exists—the heart. Sexual struggles have a much deeper beginning point than your eyes and your sexual organs.

So if sexual problems are problems of the heart, it's important to make some biblical observations about the heart. I'm persuaded that you can't have a conversation about the sexual insanity that's around and in us and will lead to real person change without these heart principles from Scripture.

1) You need to know what the Bible is talking about when it talks about the heart.

Scripture presents the heart as the seat of our emotion, motivation, will, thought, and desire. What this means is that when you encounter the word "heart" in your Bible you should have the following definition in your brain. The heart is the *causal center of your personhood*. This means that people do what they do because of what's in their hearts. Situations don't cause you to do what you do. People don't cause you to do what you do. Locations don't cause you to do what you do. Your heart does. That's the Bible's humbling bottom line. Inside of you is a control center; it's called the heart.

2) You need to understand that the heart is always functioning under the rule of something.

The heart is a control center.

3) You need to realize that the heart is the worship center.

Your heart is always submitting to the rulership of something. And there are only two possibilities. Your heart functions under the control of the Creator or the creation. Now, this is more helpful than it may at first seem. It isn't wrong to desire pleasure, but if you love pleasure more than you love God, you're a person heading for trouble. It isn't wrong to enjoy comfort, but if your heart is more controlled by desire for comfort than by love for God, you're heading somewhere not good. You see, the problem is not that your heart has the capacity to desire; the problem is ruling desire. Let me say it as I've said it before: *the desire for even a good thing becomes a bad thing when that desire becomes a ruling thing.* When the pleasures of sex exercise more control over your heart than the will of God does, your heart has already stepped beyond God's boundaries, and your body will soon follow.

4) You need to realize that what controls your heart will direct your behavior.

Your behavior is inextricably connected to the thoughts and desires of your heart. This means that people and situations never cause you to do what you do. People and situations may be the occasion and location of what you do, but never the cause. So when you have done with sex what God says that you should not do, you can't look outside of yourself for explanations. You must look inside of yourself. If, as Jesus says, you've already committed adultery in your heart, it won't be long before you commit the act with the members of your body. Here's what these two diagnostic passages tell us: it is always the sin of thought and desire in your heart that hooks you to the evil in the world in which you live. Your problem when it comes to sex is much deeper than an entertainment and media culture that has simply gone crazy. Your problem is the self-oriented, pleasure-addicted insanity that lives inside of you and makes you an easy target for the madness of the society around you. Monasteries and boycotts simply don't create pure living; never have, never will.

5) You need to realize that this side of eternity your heart is susceptible.

Because of all that I wrote in the paragraph above, you and I must humbly admit that we live in a constant state of susceptibility. None of us has a pure heart. You read it right—not one of us. Yes, by the grace of the cross, the power of sin has been broken, but that doesn't mean we are sin-free. No, sin still lives with deceptive and destructive power in each one of our hearts, and its hold over our hearts is being progressively eradicated by God's sanctifying grace. I'd like to think that I am one of the pure ones, but I give regular empirical evidence that I'm not. All of us carry impure desires inside of us. All of us think impure thoughts. We all dream impure dreams. We all crave what we shouldn't crave. All of us. This side of heaven, complete moral purity is a self-righteous delusion that we would all do well to reject. Our hearts continue to be dark and messy as grace continues to work to purify us.

There is not a moment in your life when you are not susceptible because, admit it, there are still areas where you want what you should not want. In silence, secrecy, or a lack of self-knowledge, you look at things in a way that you should not look, you begin to consider what you should not consider, and you entertain dreams that you should not entertain. You're in the process of offering up your susceptible heart, all the while telling yourself that you are pure.

6) You need to admit that this side of eternity your heart is fickle.

I get uncomfortable in those worship-service moments when we are singing, "You are my all in all," You're my priceless treasure," 'With all my heart I love you," or "I adore you." I often stop singing and think, "Really? Do I?" Does love of God rule my heart unchallenged? Does it? Is God at the center of my affections, the focus of my greatest joys? Really, is he? I think we seriously underestimate the fickle nature of our sinful hearts. We quickly switch loyalties. We rapidly trade affection for one thing for another. We all too easily give way to our love. We willingly abandon commitments we forcefully made. We fail to do what we promised. We abandon our dreams for what we think would be a better dream. Our hearts will only ever be truly loyal and stable when our hearts are sin-free. As long as sin lives inside of us in some way, we're all sadly shopping for a better, more satisfying master, denying the glory of the Master that by grace we've been given.

7) You need to face the fact that this side of eternity your heart is deceptive.

We would all like to think that no one knows our hearts better than we do. We would like to believe that others may be self-deceived, but we are not. It's simply not true. Since sin is in its essence deceptive, as long as sin lives in our hearts, we will tend to be blind to the true condition of our hearts. But more must be said. Not only will we be blind to our hearts; we will be blind to our blindness, thinking we see when we really don't. To add to this, we will participate in our own blindness. Because of the self-righteousness of sin, we will work to make ourselves feel good about what is not good or to believe that the problem is not, in fact, us. So the man who has looked too long at the woman at work in a way that he should not, will tell himself that it is not lust, that he's just one of those guys who notices the beauty of God's creation. ("Is it a sin to recognize when a woman is beautiful?") A relationship that has grown emotional and a bit physical will be characterized as a close friendship ("Is it wrong to have close female friends?) A woman who has begun to emotionally replace her husband will say she needs friendships with other men in her life. ("Is it wrong for a married woman to hear the perspectives of another man?") Each question is a self-atoning question. Each person is a participant in the deception of his or her own heart. Since the heart is deceptive, we are often in sexual danger long before our eyes see it and our heart admits it.

8) You need to face the fact that your body will
wander where your heart has already gone.

I don't need to say much more about this; I said much already. I think, though, that this point needs to be highlighted. Sexual problems are symptomatic of deeper problems of the heart, and if you give away your heart you simply will not be successful in controlling your body.

9) You need to confess that your behavior always
reveals more about you than it does about your
situation, location, or relationships.

It is here, I think, that the evangelical church has tended to lack honesty, integrity, and biblical accuracy. When it comes to the growing sexual insanity that exist in our churches (How much Internet pornography? How much marital adultery? How many singles having sex? etc.), we have tended to point our fingers in the wrong direction. We have talked much about the shocking sexual degradation and coarseness of the surrounding culture. And it is shocking. We talk about the sexual images that it is almost impossible to protect our children from. We point to the sexualization of the fashion and entertainment industries. And we should talk about those things. We talk about how the Internet has been morally kidnapped by a global, multi-billion-dollar pornography empire. We talk about the moral insanity of high school health classes. We talk about how sexual humor infects even the family sitcom. All of these things are issues and need discussion and action, but self-delusion and self-righteousness make the conversation hard and set us up for greater difficulty.

When we talk about the massive indebtedness of the church, we tend to point the finger at the materialism of the surrounding culture. We talk about the fact that we are constantly being sold something. We talk about the high cost of daily living. We talk about credit cards with exorbitant fees that are all too easy to obtain. We talk about a society that is so crass as to attach the identity of a person to the labels he wears and the kind of car he drives. These too are important discussions for us to have, but they are inadequate and can also be dangerously self-righteous.

The sexual madness that lives in the seats of our Sunday services exposes and indicts the true condition of our hearts. The debt and materialism that live in our congregations reveal more about us than about the surrounding culture. Here's what's important about this chapter: when you tell yourself that the problem is not you, when you deny the centrality of your heart in every choice and action you make, and when you minimize the dangerous impurity that still lives inside of you, you don't seek the help that you desperately need, and you don't set up the protections that are clearly called for. Because of this, you set yourself up to be seduced and deceived once again.

SO, WHAT NOW?

Well, we must all face the fact that changes in our personal worlds of sex and money don't begin with cultural analysis; they begin with personal confession. Change doesn't begin with pointing to how difficult your situation is or to the behavior of the people around you. Change begins in one place: with confession that is heart deep. When it comes to sex, we all need to say that the biggest problem in our sexual lives is us. When it comes to money, we must all admit that the biggest money danger is us. It is only in these humble confessions that lasting change takes place.

I would challenge you to pray with me David's prayer of humble confession (Psalm 51). Do it right here, right now.

> Have mercy on me, O God,
>   according to your steadfast love;
> according to your abundant mercy
>   blot out my transgressions.
> Wash me thoroughly from my iniquity,
>   and cleanse me from my sin!
>
> For I know my transgressions,
>   and my sin is ever before me.
> Against you, you only, have I sinned
>   and done what is evil in your sight,
> so that you may be justified in your words
>   and blameless in your judgment.
> Behold, I was brought forth in iniquity,
>   and in sin did my mother conceive me.
> Behold, you delight in truth in the inward being,
>   and you teach me wisdom in the secret heart.
>
> Purge me with hyssop, and I shall be clean;
>   wash me, and I shall be whiter than snow.
> Let me hear joy and gladness;
>   let the bones that you have broken rejoice.
> Hide your face from my sins,
>   and blot out all my iniquities.
> Create in me a clean heart, O God,
>   and renew a right spirit within me.
> Cast me not away from your presence,
>   and take not your Holy Spirit from me.
> Restore to me the joy of your salvation,
>   and uphold me with a willing spirit.
>
> Then I will teach transgressors your ways,
>   and sinners will return to you.

Deliver me from bloodguiltiness, O God,
  O God of my salvation,
  and my tongue will sing aloud of your righteousness.
O Lord, open my lips,
  and my mouth will declare your praise.
For you will not delight in sacrifice, or I would give it;
  you will not be pleased with a burnt offering.
The sacrifices of God are a broken spirit;
  a broken and contrite heart, O God, you will not despise.

Do good to Zion in your good pleasure;
  build up the walls of Jerusalem;
then will you delight in right sacrifices,
  in burnt offerings and whole burnt offerings;
  then bulls will be offered on your altar.

You see, if our sex and money problems are a matter of our hearts, if it is true that we do what we do because of what's in our hearts, then we need something more than cultural analysis, biblical information, and rules. Give a man who is addicted to Internet pornography a set of rules and see how far that takes him. Give a person who is in deep debt a budget and see how long it is before he is once again in debt. Sexual sin is a matter of the heart. Debt is an attitude of the heart. Our only hope for personal purity and for a defense against cultural insanity is found in the transformation of our hearts, and for that we need the very same mercy for which David cries out in this beautiful, heart-wrenching psalm.

Won't you stop right now and cry out for the very same grace? You need it right now as much as David did, whether or not you admit that to yourself.

4

THE HIGHEST PLEASURE

The multi-layered beauty of a sunset.

The sweet song of a bird.

The biting herbaceousness of cilantro.

The tender delicacy of a human kiss.

The whistle of the breeze through leaves of a giant oak.

The cacophony of sound that is the animal kingdom.

The shimmer of a glassy, still pond.

The variegated beauty of the human form.

The gorgeous aroma of a rose.

The seemingly endless catalog of herbs and spices.

The emotional power of music.

The communicative power of visual art.

The gift of eyes, ears, mouth, nose, and hands to take it all in.

The existence of the desire for pleasure.

The ability to recognize and enjoy beauty.

The capacity to create beauty.

The endless sights, sounds, shapes, colors, light, and textures of the created world.

The sedentary pleasure of sleep.

The fact that all of this and more is available to us everyday. The pleasures of life are everywhere you turn. They greet you every day and all throughout the day. You couldn't escape pleasure if you tried. Do you know why? There is only one answer:

because God wanted it that way. With wisdom and purpose, he created a world that is stuffed to overflowing with pleasures of every kind. There are pleasures of sight, sound, taste, and touch. There are pleasures of thought and emotion. There are pleasures of location, situation, and relationship. Pleasure exists because it fits with God's purpose for his creation. It is one of his chief gifts to us. But you and I need to understand the role of pleasure in God's creation and how we are to respond to the pleasures that greet us every day.

Let me start by noting this: you simply cannot write a book about sex and money and avoid the larger topic of pleasure. Maybe the best way to say it is this: if you get pleasure wrong, you tend to misuse both sex and money. So before we begin to look at sex and money more specifically and in much greater detail, it is vital that we address the core issue of both—pleasure.

THE BIRTH OF PLEASURE

It is not an overstatement of a distant theological platitude to say that pleasure and its birth are in the mind of God. Legitimate pleasure of any type is God's creation, and our ability to recognize and enjoy pleasure is the result of his design. There is no better place to see this and to trace its implications than to go back to the beginning, to the garden of Eden. I want to introduce you to the *Eden hermeneutic*. Hermeneutics is the science of interpretation. You and I don't live life based on the facts of our existence but on our unique and personal interpretation of the facts. Here's how it works for our topic: if God created pleasure, then pleasure is not the problem. The problem comes when we understand pleasure in the wrong way and then involve ourselves in pleasure in ways that are the direct result of the wrong interpretations we have made.

So, like everything else, when it comes to pleasure we need some kind of interpretive guide, and God's creation of the garden of Eden and the placing of Adam and Eve in it provide the perfect interpretive tool for us. Let me suggest five critical perspectives on pleasure that emerge as you look at it through the interpretive window of the garden.

1) The ascetics have it wrong.

Asceticism (from the Greek word for "training" or "exercise") has been around for a long time and still exists in various forms in evangelical Christianity. The chief worldview of the ascetic is that by renouncing worldly pleasures you can achieve a higher spiritual state. The problem with asceticism is that it misunderstands the nature of God's creation and the nature of human beings and, in so doing, makes pleasure the problem. The existence of the garden of Eden in a world of perfection simply blows asceticism away.

God didn't cruelly place Adam and Eve in an environment of dangerous and evil pleasure and then require then to avoid it in fear of their destruction and his judgment. He didn't require abstinence as a true test of the loyalty and godliness of their hearts. No, the opposite is true. He placed them in an environment of delicious pleasures and set them free to enjoy. The garden was full of the pleasures of sight, sound, smell, touch, and taste. The garden introduced them to the pleasures of emotional and sexual love. It was a gloriously pleasurable place to live, and there was simply nothing inherently evil or dangerous in any of it. Being what God created Adam and Eve to be did not demand avoidance; it required participation. Asceticism is wrong because it curses creation and assesses holiness by the degree of your separation from creation. This doesn't put God in his rightful place. It does just the opposite. It views him as either cruel or unwise or both. It presents him not as one you want to run to but rather as one to protect yourself from.

Asceticism also misunderstands the nature of human beings. It gets to the heart of what I have given myself to write about. Human beings are inside-out beings. That is, we do what we do not so much because of what is outside of us but because of what is inside of us. If God had created people whose choices and behavior were hopelessly determined by what was outside of them, he surely wouldn't have placed them in this environment of such gorgeous delights. They would've been quickly overwhelmed and soon addicted, unable to control themselves because of the powerful determinants that were everywhere around them.

But Adam and Eve weren't made like that. They were given hearts that could think, imagine, consider, weigh, choose, feel, regret, and worship. And God knew that as long as their hearts were not controlled by pleasure but ruled by him, they would be able to engage in pleasure in a way that brought him glory and didn't result in their losing their way.

The creation of the garden of delights and the tragedy of the rebellion of Genesis 3 come together to tell us this one vital thing: pleasure isn't your problem; you are. It sounds unkind, doesn't it? But it's true. All pleasure problems are heart problems. We haven't gone sex-and-money insane because sex and money exist. Rather, our sex-and-money insanity reveals the disloyalty and rebellion of our hearts. So you don't deal with sex-and-money problems by naming them as evil things to be avoided. It's not unspiritual to have lots and lots of money. It is not worldly to really enjoy sex (in its God-ordained context). Poor people simply aren't closer to God, and celibate people aren't spiritual nobility.

The garden says it all. Separating yourself from the very pleasures that point to God's glory and were given to you to enjoy doesn't solve the pleasure problem. Rather, it blames the thing and calls into question the wisdom and love of the one who created it.

2) Pleasure is God-glorifying.

God's creative intention was to bring glory to himself by the pleasures that he created. Each pleasurable thing was perfectly created and designed to reflect and point to the greater glory of the one who created it. These things were designed not only to be pleasure inducing but also for a deeply spiritual purpose. They were meant to remind you of him. They were meant to amaze you not just with their existence but with the wisdom, power, and glory of the one who made them. They were put on earth to be one of God's means of getting your attention and capturing your heart.

You see, you will never understand pleasure if you think that it is an end in itself. Pleasure is pleasurable, and you should never feel guilty that you have enjoyed its pleasure or that you want more. This is all according to God's design. But you and I must understand that pleasure has a purpose beyond the momentary enjoyment it will give us. Pleasure exists as a sign of the existence of one in whose arms I will enjoy the only pleasure that can satisfy and give rest to my heart. Pleasure exists to put God in my face and remind me that I was made by him and for him. Pleasure, like every other created thing was designed to put God at the center, not just of my physical joy but of the deepest thoughts and motives of my heart. Pleasure exists to stimulate worship, not of the thing but of the one who created the thing. The glory of every form of pleasure is meant to point me to the glory of God.

The pleasure of sex is meant to remind me of the glory of my intimate union with Christ that only grace could produce. The pleasure of food is meant to motivate me to seek the heart-satisfying sustenance of the bread and wine that is Christ. The pleasure of all things beautiful is designed to cause me to gaze upon the Lord, who is perfect in beauty in every way. The pleasure of sound is meant to cause me to listen to the sounds of the one whose every utterance is a thing of beauty. The pleasure of touch was created to remind me of the glory of one whose touch alone has the power to comfort, heal, and transform. The pleasure of human affection is meant to induce me to celebrate the glory of God's eternal, underserved, self-sacrificing love. The pleasure of rest is meant to draw my heart toward the one who in his life, death, and resurrection purchased for me an eternal sabbath of rest.

Pleasure doesn't detract from God's glory. It doesn't necessarily deaden your heart. Rather, it is one of God's means of reminding you of the satisfying glories that can only be found in him. Pleasure in Eden and now, like every other created thing, was created to lead you and me to worship.

3) Pleasure demands boundaries.

It is important to recognize that the pleasures of the garden weren't boundless. God set boundaries for Adam and Eve. He gifted them with glorious pleasures to be enjoyed but within the limits that he set. They were not to have a self-centered, anytime-anyway relationship to pleasure. They were designed and called to live inside of the purpose that God had in mind for them when he made them. Their lives did not belong to them, and neither did their pleasures. They were free to enjoy, but their enjoyment was to be done in an attitude of submission and obedience. The boundaries were a protection. The rules themselves let Adam and Eve know that they weren't in charge. The rules reminded them that they were created for the purposes of another.

The rules weren't pleasure destroying or enjoyment inhibiting. The rules were there to protect the hearts of Adam and Eve so they would be free to liberally enjoy the pleasures of the created world without being dominated, addicted, or controlled by them. The rules were there so they wouldn't give themselves to pleasure but to God, as they enjoyed the beautiful things he had provided for them. Isn't this a key place where our culture simply gets it wrong? There is an overarching philosophy in Western culture that tells us that authority destroys freedom and rules wreck pleasure. It's the "pleasure isn't really pleasurable when there are rules attached to it" worldview that has been a key ingredient in the insanity that this book is written to address. This view says that eating is no fun if you're being told what to eat. Sex is not enjoyable if you're being told how, when, and who you can have it with. Money is not pleasurable if you're required to spend it in certain ways. Creating things of beauty is not satisfying and pleasurable if you have to think about the message communicated by what you create. Eden was the most beautiful place that ever existed, filled with perfect pleasures of every kind, yet its continuance depended on Adam and Eve staying inside of God's protective boundaries. It's the horror of the human existence that they decided not to. Boundless pleasure is a deception. By God's design it doesn't exist, and if it did it could never work.

4) Your life of pleasure is protected only by pleasure.

Your heart and mine will be controlled by some kind of pleasure. When your heart is ruled by the desire for a particular kind of pleasure, you cannot stop thinking about it, you can't shut off your desire for it, so you will do anything you can to get it. This is a dangerous place to be, and it is a destructive way to live. So if a man's heart is ruled by sexual pleasure, he will put wonderful things in his life at risk in pursuit of this thing that he is convinced he cannot live without. Or if someone's heart is ruled by the pleasure of food, he will eat the wrong things way too often and in much too great a quantity. Meanwhile he will ignore the empirical evidence of weight gain, hypertension, and diabetes that are God-given warning signs that he is serving the wrong master.

It is only when your heart is mastered by the one who created all the pleasures that can so easily addict that your world of pleasure is protected and can live in balance. It is only when your heart is controlled by a higher pleasure, the pleasure of God, that you can handle pleasure without being addicted to it. It is only when what gives the greatest pleasure in life is the knowledge that God is pleased by the way you are living that you will handle pleasure properly. If the only thing in life that motivates you is that you would be pleased, you are in pleasure trouble, although you may not yet see the evidence of it. If your principal motive is that God would be pleased, then you can liberally enjoy the variegated pleasures of the created world without rendering yourself fat, addicted, and in debt. When the hearts of Adam and Eve began to be ruled by a pleasurable created thing and not by the one who created it, they quit caring about what pleased God, inserted themselves into the center of the world, wrote their own rules, and created the ultimate human disaster—the fall. We are still among the twisted remains of that horrible choice.

5) When it comes to pleasure, what seems good is often not good.

At some point in the conversation with the Serpent, Eve began to look at a very bad thing and saw a very good thing. But the temporary pleasure of the fruit of the forbidden tree was not a good thing for her to consume. It opened a floodgate of destruction, judgment, and death. Pleasure can be incredibly seductive. Pleasure is often deceptive. Be warned: your pleasures will tell you lies. Your pleasures will make promises they cannot fulfill. Your pleasures will offer you life when in fact they will deliver to you the opposite.

When you are committing an act of gluttony, at that moment you don't see the idolatrous destructiveness of what you're doing. No, you see good—the good of the smells, sights, textures, and flavors of the food you are consuming. Your problem is that what looks good isn't in fact good. When you are charging something you want, spending money you don't have, you don't see the dangers of making promises you can't keep. No, you're too taken with the delights to come to see that this good thing is really a bad thing. When you're looking at a sexual website that you have no business viewing, you don't see the selfish destructiveness of what you're doing. You are too taken with the erotic beauty of the human form to see that what looks like a good thing is really a very dangerous and destructive thing. When it comes to pleasure, what looks like a good thing may not be a good thing.

So, as you're dealing with the basic pleasures that will greet you in everyday life, carry the *Eden hermeneutic* with you. Look at pleasure through the interpretive and protective lens of the garden. Understand pleasure, be reminded of its purpose, celebrate its joys, be warned of its danger, and most of all guard your heart.

SO WHERE DO WE GO FROM HERE?

Well, there is one final, intensely practical question that needs to be asked. It gets at the heart of how good pleasures become dangerous things. It also gets at the heart of who you are and how you were designed by God to function. Here's the question: what are you asking of your pleasure? You have been designed by God for pleasure. You have been placed by God in a pleasure-saturated world. You have been hardwired with the senses to take in and enjoy the pleasures that are around you. In short, you are a pleasure seeker. The issue for you is what kind of pleasures will you give your heart to, and what will you ask of those pleasures?

The good pleasures that God created for our enjoyment and for his glory become bad and dangerous things when we ask those pleasures to do for us what they were not intended by God to do. For example, if sex becomes a way you establish power, you will do things in sex that you should not do, you will use others as objects of your power, and you will leave behind you a trail of destruction while you do damage to your own heart. God didn't give you the gift of the pleasure of sex in order for you to establish personal power and control. I worked in an institution for troubled boys where that was exactly how sex was used. Same-sex rape was a way that older boys established dominance over younger, weaker boys. It was a dark and violent distortion of the pleasurable gift of human sexuality.

If you use the pleasure of money and what it can purchase for you as a way of getting identity, you will tend to deny who you really are, you will tend to buy into the delusion that you are what you own, you will tend to purchase what you do not really need, and you will be left spending more than you can afford.

If you use wine, which is not in itself an evil thing, as a means of escape from the pressures of life, you are asking wine to do for you what it was not created to do. If wine is your spiritual refuge, you will drink more than you should and, in so doing, compound your problems, while finding neither solutions nor rest for your heart.

There are two observations that flow out of the questions we are considering. The first is that in each instance people are *asking the wrong thing* of pleasure. They are asking it to do the one thing that it can never do—satisfy their hearts. The pleasures that God created and embedded in the world that he made for us were never intended to be where you and I look for identity, inner rest, contentment, or the stability of well-being that every human being seeks. Pleasure will never be your savior. There is a loving, capable, and willing Savior who offers you in his grace everything you need. Pleasure can offer you momentary joy. It can remind you of the greater glory of God, but it must never become your functional God-replacement.

The second observation is that in each instance people are *asking in the wrong way*. The basic approach of people to sex, money, and alcohol puts them in the center of their world. It's a "what I want and what I think I need" approach to life. It doesn't submit to the reality that all pleasure belongs to the Lord. It fails to remember that pleasure had its beginning in the mind of God. It ignores the fact that, like everything else God created, he has a specific purpose for pleasure. So this approach fails to live willingly and joyfully inside of God boundaries.

This way of living descends to the level of "I have a right to be happy and the right to pursue the pleasures that deliver it to me." No matter what the confessional theology of the moment, it is a God-ignoring way of living that inserts me in the center of my world, that makes my personal definition of happiness paramount, that gives me the right to write my own rules, and that completely forgets the eternally satisfying pleasures of the love of God that only grace can deliver to me. And it denies the reality that asking pleasure to do what it was not intended to do never goes anywhere good. When I live for the short-term buzz of any pleasure, because it cannot give me lasting satisfaction I go back again and again, each time wanting more and better, so finding myself controlled by what I once could control. I look around one day, and I'm addicted and enslaved, and the bondage is not something that pleasure did to me. No, sadly it's something that I did to me when I decided to ask something that was designed to remind me of my Savior to be my savior.

WHILE YOU'RE CELEBRATING PLEASURE, CELEBRATE THE CROSS

It's right to celebrate the goodness of God in giving you sweet pleasures in life to enjoy, and you should never feel guilty in enjoying them as long as you do it within his boundaries and for his glory. It's wonderful to celebrate the tasty pleasures of food, the stunning beauty of a fine piece of art, the sweet intimacy of sex, or the sound drama of a well-written piece of music. But as you're celebrating pleasure, don't forget to celebrate grace.

It's God's grace that has the power to protect you from asking of pleasure what you should not ask. It's God's grace that gives you the power to say no to the seductive call of pleasure when it is vital for you to say no. It's God grace that offers you forgiveness when you have failed to do both of these things. And its grace that ushers you into the presence of the one who alone can give you the lasting satisfaction and joy that your heart seeks. So as you're celebrating the physical pleasures of the created world that God has given you, take time to celebrate the eternal pleasures of redemption. And remember to celebrate the fact that as God's child you are heading to a place where pleasure will no longer have any danger attached to it and where your restful heart will not seek what it should not seek.

So when you've had a good meal, your bank account has grown, or you've enjoyed mutual sexual love with your spouse, don't feel guilty. God created pleasure for his glory and your joy. He surrounded you with pleasurable things. He gave you the capacity to enjoy them. You shouldn't feel guilty, but you must remember the tendency of your heart to wander, to replace the Creator with his creation. And remember that a desire for even a good thing becomes a bad thing when it becomes a ruling thing. Be faithful to remind yourself again and again that to resist being ruled by what you've been welcomed to enjoy, you have been given forgiving, empowering, transforming, and delivering grace for the battle. Few things argue more strongly for your need of that grace than your struggle to keep God-given pleasures in their proper place.

5

SEX: THE BIG PICTURE

Jim was thirteen years old and something had been awakened in him. He was not sure what it was, but he liked it. He liked it a lot. It happened to him when he looked at pictures of women in magazines. It happened to him as he walked by those lingerie stores at the mall. It happened when he quietly surfed his way onto certain websites. He felt the buzz, and he liked it. And all he knew was that it felt good, and he wanted more.

• • •

Aaron didn't really care about how comfortable his wife was. He didn't really think much about what was good and enjoyable for her. He didn't really think about the gentle, tender, relational aspect of intimacy. Aaron thought this way: "I'm married, and sex is my right, no holds barred." He felt that Ginger should be ready any time he requested sex and that she should do whatever it was that brought him pleasure. If he came home in the middle of the day and was ready, then it was her responsibility to be willing.

But Ginger felt like an object, a plaything for Aaron's pleasure. She felt put upon and demanded of. Sex was less and less for her an act of mutual love. It had become a daily obligation, one she increasingly dreaded. And to make matters worse she was uncomfortable with the things that Aaron was asking her to do, not to mention the fear she had that sex seemed to be a growing obsession for him. She had tried to get Aaron to talk with her about their sexual life, but he told her he thought everything was cool. She had tried to share her feelings with him, but he didn't seem to listen. She had tried refusing his advances at points, but he only got angry and accused her of being selfish. Aaron was demanding what Ginger dreaded, and she just didn't know what to do.

• • •

Mandy was in college and she loved every minute of the experience. For the first time in her life she felt independent and attractive. She loved the attention she was getting from the guys in her dorm and in her classes. Her first two years had been a whirlwind of classes, dating, and short-term romances. She was maintaining her grades and occasionally thought about her future, but that's not what kept her going; the social scene was. Her weekends began on Thursday night and didn't end until Sunday very late. On Monday the plan for the next weekend was already forming.

Mandy loved the fact that she didn't feel awkward any more. She liked the way her body had developed, and she liked the fact that her looks got her lots of male attention. She felt alive and appreciated. Although she was uncomfortable with some of the things her romantic partners wanted her to do, she loved that she was so attractive that guys were always after her.

In ways that Mandy was not conscious of, she didn't so much dress to cover or adorn her body as to expose and draw attention to it. Mandy was not scared about being thought of as a slut. What really scared her was that any of the guys around her would think of her as a prude. With makeup too heavy and clothes too tight she would begin each day expecting and reveling in the attention she got as she made her way around the campus. Her way of responding to the guys around her was flirtatious and seductive, but she would deny it if you said that to her. She saw herself as a normal twenty-year-old girlie girl getting in touch with her emotions and her body. If asked about her lifestyle she would say, "Lots of fun, little harm."

• • •

Gerrard had made the decision, and for him there was no turning back. He told himself that he was simply being true to his feeling, true to the way he had been put together. He knew his parents would be upset, but he was tired of living in the shadows and covering his tracks. He wasn't going to do it anymore. He knew what turned him on and what didn't. He knew who he was attracted to and who he wasn't. He knew the kind of life he wanted and the one he wanted to avoid. With his decision made, he felt quite liberated.

Gerrard was attracted to men. He told himself that he had always been that way. He had come to see denying it as stupid and immature. And he thought the people around him had no right to question it. And he was convinced it was a colossal waste of time to fight it. This weekend, while with his parents, he was going to declare his sexual orientation and his love for David. He didn't want to needlessly hurt his parents, but they would just have to come to terms with who he was and how he had decided to live his life. He thought of himself as a Christian, but he had little time for what the Bible had to say about his lifestyle choice. He wasn't going to bow to the "ancient chauvinism of biblical times." He said he loved God, and he was content with the kind of person that God had made him to be. He didn't feel the need to change anything.

• • •

Teddy hated old age, and he hated being alone. He hated not having a companion to share his life with, but if he were able to be honest, what he really hated was the loss of his sexual life. He couldn't stop thinking about it. It made no sense to him, and it made him bitter. He was fully alive and virile but had no sex in his future. It made no sense that God would design him, give him this kind of body and these kinds of desires, but forbid him to express them simply because his wife had died and he was alone. What was he supposed to do with his feeling and his urges? "Yes, I'm old, but I'm not dead," he would say to himself.

He envied the young couples at church and fantasized what sex was like for them. He looked at the younger women at his church and wondered if any of them would ever be attracted to him. He felt that his life at this point was a sick joke or maybe a divine punishment of some kind. He couldn't image continuing to live like this. He'd rather be dead.

• • •

Heather had no sexual attraction to her husband whatsoever. Since they had gotten married he had put on about 35 pounds. The athletic body of the man she married had given way to this pudgy guy who spent most of his time at home sitting in warm-ups watching the sports he no longer had the energy to play. When Heather saw his body, she was turned off by what she saw. When they attempted to have sex, all she could think of was the size of his belly. She would occasionally succumb to his advances, but it was all she could do to fake her way through and make sure that he was satisfied enough to leave her alone for a few days.

Heather fantasized about being married to a fit and handsome man. She dreamed about having sex with someone and feeling his muscles, not his flab. She was unhappy, and she felt trapped. It all made her angry. She couldn't imagine living the rest of her life this way. She had sexual desires that needed to be satisfied, but not by Lumpy (the rather cruel nickname that Heather had given her husband). If fact, when she had sex with her husband, Heather would often find her way through it by fantasizing that she was with someone else. She found herself absorbing more of the romance novels that seemed to be everywhere. She built this vicarious sexual life, living in worlds of attraction and seduction that didn't exist but that took her away from the prison that she had gotten herself into.

There was no self-conscious, point-in-time decision, but Heather began to plan her escape. She thought about what she would say to her husband and how she would break the news to her family. She wondered how she would support herself and where she would live. She worried about whether there would be a big battle for the kids. She wanted to feel attractive again, and she wanted to be attracted to someone once again. She wanted sex where she could give herself, not pretend that she was doing that. She was tired of doing things that revolted her with someone who repulsed her. And Heather just couldn't imagine that this is the way God wanted her to live. She didn't know how, and she hadn't yet considered when, but she knew that somehow, someway she was getting out.

LITTLE-PICTURE SEX

All of the people about whom I have just written are suffering from the same thing. It is more powerful than they know; it has made sex to be something that it isn't and has created deep dissatisfaction in all of them. What shapes, controls, and ultimately distorts their sexuality, making a beautiful thing a dark and painful thing, is *little-picture sex*.

Sex is not a thing unto itself that can exist by itself. Sex, by design, is meant to be connected. It is meant to be tied to and understood in relation to big things of huge and consequential proportion. *Big-picture sex* is sex that is understood as being part of how life was designed and what it is meant to be. *Little-picture sex*, because it is isolated, gets kidnapped by desires and agendas that rob it of its original purpose. *Big-picture sex* acknowledges that there is something bigger than personal physical pleasure.

Little-picture sex exists in the small confines of what will give me pleasure at this point in my life. *Big-picture sex* serves something bigger. *Little picture sex* is owned by the individual and is entitled and demanding. *Big-picture sex* willing submits to rules. *Little-picture sex* writes its own rules. *Big-picture sex* is driven by a commitment to others. *Little-picture sex* is dominated by the pleasures of self. *Big-pictures sex* is patient and kind. *Little-picture sex* makes impatient demands and punishes you when you don't come through. *Big-picture sex* is viewed as a part of life. *Little-picture sex* tends to take over your life. *Big-picture sex* contributes to deeper love and worship. *Little-picture sex* leads to relational hurt and vertical rebellion. God designed sex to be inextricably connected to things of consequence. It doesn't work any other way.

OUR SEX PROBLEMS AREN'T FIRST PHYSICAL

My wife, Luella, and I love art museums. We love post-war abstraction. We love what shape, color, texture, and light can communicate when juxtaposed in a way that is interesting, provocative, or beautiful. I had seen details of a work we had gone to see, and I wasn't really that impressed. (A detail is a section of a painting that is used for announcement and advertising purposes.) The artist was one of the greats, so I was willing to go check out the exhibit anyway. When I saw the painting from which they had taken the detail, I was blown away. I couldn't stop looking at it. The detail had melted into the painting—it wasn't the thing that stood out—but the painting would not have looked the same without it.

So it is with sex. When it exists as an isolated, disconnected part of our lives, it not only loses its contextual beauty but begins to be known and understood as something that it's not. Here's why human sexuality must be understood and experienced from the vantage point of the *big picture*. You and I simply need to humbly admit that the things that make sex gorgeous, exciting, and fulfilling as per God's design are not natural and intuitive to us. It's intuitive to be self-oriented, entitled, and demanding. It's natural to want to write our own rules. It's normal to act as if our bodies belong to us. It's intuitive to think that the goal of life is to experience our personal definition of happiness and pleasure. It's natural to see others as a means of our being happy. It's normal to think of life in physical and material terms. It's intuitive to live for the moment. It's intuitive to practically forget God's existence and to live a life that is dominated by horizontal concerns. It's natural to try to work the people around us into a willingness to deliver to us what would make us happy. It's comfortable to think more in terms of "I want" than "I should." You see, what distorts sex, what has the power to make it hurtful and dark, is not first the physical demands we make on one another or the way we physically use one another. What puts sex on a pathway that it was never meant to travel is something deeply spiritual. Our biggest sex problems lurk inside of us; they're not the result of a culture that has gone sexually insane. The culture has become sexually insane because of what lurks inside of us.

Now, I know that this will be a struggle for some of you to get on board with. I know it will make some of you angry, and some of you will read with hurt feelings, but what I'm about to say needs to be said. What I just described above are the normal characteristics of *little-picture sex*. They are also the very things that twist and distort the beautiful creation of God and press it into something that it was never intended to be. Yes, *little-picture sex* is still sex, but it is carnival-mirror, distorted sex. So here's the humbling admission: apart from God's grace rescuing us from us, the things that are natural and intuitive to us are the very things that rust and ruin sex. You see, none of us come to sex with neutral hearts. None of us approach sex free of the me-ism of the sinful nature. None of us comes to sex morally pure. None of us is free from the temptation to insert ourselves in the middle of our worlds, making it all about us. None of us. You can't just run with what is natural, because what is natural to you as a sinner will invariably start you in a different direction from what the Creator designed as good.

Sex exposes our hearts, and in exposing our hearts, sex reminds us of how deep and comprehensive our need is for God's forgiving, transforming, and ultimately delivering grace. In his grace God has entered our struggle with sex and done two things for us. First, he has given us the big picture. It's that 30,000-foot view of life that is the grand sweep of Scripture. In this way the Bible doesn't simply define the religious domain of our life; it redefines and reorients every single thing in our life, including our sexuality. But God has done more than just that, as important as his Word is. He gave us Jesus, who entered our struggle, lived as we couldn't live, died the death we should have died, and rose, defeating death, so that we would have everything we need to live as God intended—yes, live as God intended, even in our sexual lives.

SO WHAT DOES BIG-PICTURE SEX LOOK LIKE?

As I stated before, *big-picture sex* is connected sex. And what is it connected to? It is connected to the things that God lovingly reveals in his Word as being vital and important. If you don't look at sex (or anything else in your life) through the lens of these things, then whatever you're looking at you haven't seen correctly. If your way of thinking about your own sexuality or if your sexual desires or your definition of good sex doesn't include these things, then your thinking will be inherently wrong at some point or at some level. Let's consider these things.

1) Sex is connected to God's existence.

Since God created both you and sex, it is impossible to properly understand sex and participate in it appropriately if you are practically ignoring God and his existence. By means of creation you are his, and your sex life is his. This means that you do not have a natural right to do with your life and your body as you please. You are not entitled to an autonomous pursuit of happiness. In fact, you don't have autonomy. Your life came from him and belongs to him. Sex connects you to God, whether or not you recognize it. The way you express your sexuality either will recognize God's existence and honor him or will deny his existence and rebel against his authority. If the latter, then sex will reveal that you think you have liberty that you do not have, rights that you have never been given, and authority that only ever belongs to the Creator.

Sex that recognizes God's existence becomes the beautiful, intimate, relational act of worship that it was intended to be. In the midst of all its physical delights, it does not forget God. It remembers that everything enlivened and enjoyed in sex belongs to him. It rests in his control and celebrates his care in the midst of the most intimate of human connections. I will say much more about this in chapters to come.

2) Sex is connected to God's glory.

Creation isn't ultimate. The joys of creation were designed by God to be enjoyable, but that joy wasn't designed to be ultimate. All the joys of creation are meant to direct you toward greater joy. All the glories of the created world are meant to produce in you a hunger for greater glory and to point you to where that glory can be found. All the intimate physical and emotional glories of sex are meant to point you to the one glory for which you were created to live and through which your heart will be fulfilled.

Now, this immediately tells you two very practical things. First, sex cannot and will not ever satisfy your heart. The purpose of sex is not to bring you to a point of spiritual satisfaction. Maybe you're thinking, "Paul, what in the world are you talking about? Nobody hopes sex will do that." In fact, I am convinced that many, many people do. They look for sex to do something for them that it was never designed to do. I counseled a woman who said she had had sex with at least a hundred men, and she told me that she would do anything (sexual) to hear a man whisper in her ear, "I love you." Do you see what she was doing? She was hoping to get identity, value, and that inner sense of peace through sex. Sex couldn't do for her what she wanted it to do, so she had to go back again and again, each time getting further from her goal. Sex would never deliver what she was asking; only the God who created sex could, and sex was created to point to him.

But there is something foundational that must be understood here. In our sexual life we must be propelled by a greater glory than our own. Sex *is* glorious, and it makes us feel powerful, connected, and alive. But we must not own these glories for ourselves alone. We were created to live in the most intimate and personal places of our lives for a glory bigger than our own, the glory of God. You may be thinking, "Like, how in the world do you do that in the middle of foreplay or intercourse?" Keep reading; the chapters that follow will unpack this even more practically.

3) Sex is connected to God's purpose.

You and I do not live by instinct. We are purpose-oriented beings by God's design. Everything you do, you do for a reason, whether or not you are aware of that. In sex you are always motivated by purpose. Perhaps your only purpose is personal erotic pleasure. Perhaps your purpose is mutual erotic satisfaction. Perhaps your purpose is more frequenct sexual intercourse. None of these things is evil in itself if it is connected to and protected by the larger purpose of God. As we said earlier, everything made by God's hands was made for a purpose. So in sex, as in everything else, you must ask, "What is God's purpose for this compelling, intimate human relationship?"

One of the reasons that sex gets distorted and becomes something God never intended it to be and ends up being hurtful, dark, and dangerous is that in this fallen world it is most often motivated by no larger purpose than the pleasure of the individual. So, selfish teenage boys coerce their girlfriends into oral sex. Materialistic women see pornography as a way of making a lot of money quickly. Married men use their wife for their pleasure with little regard for her feeling loved and cared for. Single women use their sexuality to get attention and acceptance. Unmarried people surf the Internet for sexual pleasure. Middle school boys spend secret time in the locker room making rude and immature sex jokes. Advertisers use sex to sell just about anything. Powerful men use their power to get what belongs to someone else.

Sex is only ever safe when everything we think, desire, say, and do in our sexual lives is directed and protected by the clear purpose of God as revealed in his Word, which leads us to our next point.

4) Sex is connected to God's revelation.

The God who created this world and acts to hold it together not only acts, but he speaks. He has spoken in his Word. This revelation of himself, his plan and his purpose for the world that he made, is meant to be the ultimate, overarching interpreter of life. It is in God's Word that I come to know who he is, who I am, and what in the world life is about. It is in God's Word that I learn about what sex is and who it is for. It is in God's Word that I learn the attitudes, choices, and actions that cause sex to be the holy thing that God created it to be. And it is in God's Word that I learn how sin distorts sex, what God forbids, and the temptations that must be avoided in submission to God and for the protection of self.

You could argue that the Bible is a manual on sex. To the degree that it lays out God's original purpose for sex, details how sin redirects the thoughts and motives of my heart, details what God has commanded and forbidden, offers me case studies, and points to the necessary rescue of grace—to that degree it gives me all the essential heart and life information I need to be what

I am supposed to be and do what I am supposed to do in this critical area of human life.

Sex is endangered when it is pursued outside of the critical information that you can get only through divine revelation. You cannot get it by means of individual experience or collective research. After all, God made you; he is not surprised that you are a sexual being. So as in other critical areas of your life, he has spoken to you about sex with words of wisdom and grace that you will hear nowhere else.

5) Sex is connected to God's redemption.

For us, sex always takes place between the "already" and the "not yet." Already Jesus has come, already the Word has been given, already the Spirit had been sent, but not yet has the world been restored, not yet has sin been eradicated, and not yet have you and I been finally delivered from sin. So our lives as sexual beings are always lived out in the middle of a dramatically broken world that cries out for redemption. Until this world is fully restored by its Savior Creator to the condition for which it was created, it will be a place where seductive temptations, deceit, destruction, and death still live. Your world of sexuality will be one of temptation, where deceitful voices make promises that they cannot deliver, wooing you outside of the boundaries of God's wise purpose and plan.

In this world of temptation you will see things that you were not meant to lay your eyes on. You will be told things that simply are not true. You will be offered things that you must not accept. You will be exposed to sex being used in ways it was never intended to be employed. What is dangerous will be presented you to as healthy and right, and what is wrong in the eyes of God will be held before you as right and good. What you learn about sex will be full of inaccuracies and distortions. You will barely be able to live a single day without having your morals assaulted or challenged in some way.

But there is another fundamental reality between the already and the not yet. It is that sin still lives with power inside you. Your problem is not just that you live in a broken world where temptation lurks all around you; your problem is that you are susceptible to that temptation because of the moral iniquity that still exists in your heart. I have said this before, but it bears repeating here: it is only ever the evil inside us that hooks us to the evil outside us. That is what the Bible means when it says that to the pure all things are pure.

But I am not pure. By God's grace I am growing in purity, but I'm not there yet, so I carry around in me a vulnerability to temptation. I am capable of longing for things that I should immediately resist. I am susceptible to desiring things that I should actually hate. I am tempted to look intently at what I should close my eyes to. And with all of this, I am able to swindle myself into thinking that I am okay, that what I have desired or done is not that bad after all.

You see, sex really does expose the deep and sinful selfishness of our hearts. It really does show us that at the intersection of hunger and temptation we are quite capable of being disloyal and rebellious. It does reveal that our pleasures are often more valuable to us than God's purposes. Sex does expose that desires for autonomy and self-sovereignty are still inside of us. Sex does demonstrate that I don't always love my neighbor as myself, that, in fact, I am still willing at points to use another human being for my own purposes and pleasures. Sex shows how easy it is to function as a God-amnesiac, even though in my theology I recognize his existence.

What all of this means is that sex immediately connects me to my need and the world's need for redemption. The hope for sex in human culture is not more prevalent sex education and better contraception. The hope for sex in human culture is not a thing; it is a person, and his name is Jesus. Sex groans for redemption and, in groaning for redemption, reaches out for the

Savior. And human sexuality will only ever fully be what it was intended to be when he has finally made all things new.

6) Sex is connected to God's eternity.

Finally, sex connects you to eternity and your need for the kingdom that is to come. Sex cannot be divorced from God's eternal plan. You and I must not live in this moment in time as if this is all there is. There is more and better to come. So what is this moment of sex about? This moment of sex is not a destination but part of preparing you for the final destination to come. All the struggles of sexuality are not in the way of God's plan, but part of it. God knew he was leaving us in this fallen world for a period of time. He knew well what we would face here. All the messiness between the already and the not yet is meant, in the hands of God, to be transformational. That we would through difficulty and trial became people ready for the eternity all of his redeemed children will spend with him.

But there is more. God has hardwired eternity into all of our hearts. That means there is a desire for paradise in all of us. But you will not experience paradise in the here and now. And if you try to turn this present moment into the paradise you long for, you will be anxious, controlling, disappointed, frustrated, demanding, and ultimately discouraged and bitter. Your husband or wife will never be the perfect lover. You will never experience paradise sex in the here and now. Celebrate the good things God gives you in the here and now, be content, and keep reminding yourself that you are being prepared for the wonderful eternity that is to come.

The problem is that nobody connected sex for Hank. His sexual awakening took place one afternoon when he happened upon a secret stash of '70s era girlie magazines that his father had hidden for years. He was immediately alive and magnetized. He didn't understand what had just happened to him, but he wanted more. It was a sad, seductive welcome to the world of *little-picture sex*. It was pleasure for pleasure's sake, sex for sex's sake. Over the next two years, Hank visited that hidden stash almost daily. Before long he was trying to sneak kisses from the girls at school or cop a feel where it seemed possible. He stole porn from the local newsstand and sought out art movies with nudity.

His college years consisted of sexual fantasy and sexual conquest. He probably thought about sex more than he did his studies, but he didn't see himself as in trouble. In his senior year, through a campus ministry, he made a profession of faith. He quickly learned that he could not do the things he had been doing. But his obsession did not go away, and he failed again and again. And with all the dos and don'ts that he submitted to, his view of sex was still pretty much isolated, *little-picture sex*. It makes sense that the desire for marriage would grow in Hank. It was the one place where sex was "legal," although he did not know how much that really motivated him. He also thought that getting married would solve his sex problems by giving him a place where he could be regularly satisfied.

But marriage didn't solve Hank's problem. It wasn't long before his wife felt that she was being used rather than loved, and it didn't take long for Hank to begin to live a secret life of illicit sex. When Suzy found his Internet stash, she was devastated but not surprised.

Hank then faced the depth of his need—no, not just for a more biblical sexual worldview, but his need for grace. When viewed properly, sex will always connect you to the existence and plan of God; it connects you to the fact that you and everything in your life were made for him and that you cannot be what you are supposed to be or do what you are supposed to do without his grace. Now, it may seem weird to some of you and irreverent to others, but it needs to be said. When viewed properly, sex preaches the gospel of Jesus Christ. Sex tells you how broken the world is, and it tells you how weak and rebellious you are. In telling you these things, it points you to your need for a Savior and to the hope that is found not in better education or firmer human resolve but in his forgiving, transforming, empowering, and delivering grace.

Big-picture sex acknowledges God, admits to sin, and celebrates grace and so grows in both purity and contentment. *Little-picture sex* lives in disconnected denial and never goes anywhere good. Where does your world of sexuality live?

6

IF SEX IS ABOUT WORSHIP, THEN IT CAN'T BE JUST ABOUT YOU

So where has all this sexual insanity come from? What is the root cause? Again, this insanity is not the fault of the entertainment, advertising, fashion, or Internet industries. The cause is much more foundational. Whether it's the executive who uses sex to sell a product and increase his bottom line and personal success, the teenager using sex for another immature thrill, the old man grabbing at his nurse, the young woman who uses sex to get inside the riches of an old man, the husband having sex with someone other than his wife, or the ratings-obsessed TV executive throwing sex into a sitcom even though it is not necessary to the plotline, each person is doing the same thing. In ways that they do not understand they are part of the insanity. In fact, there is something each of them is doing that drives the sexual insanity we find everywhere around us.

All of them are taking sex for their own, acting as if it belongs to them and using it for whatever purpose they choose. Sex becomes their possession, their product, and their tool. It's a "sex is all about me" view of human sexuality. I am deeply persuaded that the insanity of sex that marks human culture is the direct result of the *individualization* of sex. It's sex for my purpose, my pleasure, according to my plan. This is what the next three chapters will address. Sex according to God's wise and gracious design simply cannot be just about me. This *individualization* of sex cannot work. It will never result in sex being what God intended it to be. It will never keep sex from distortion and darkness. It will never protect sex from misuse and abuse. *Individualized* sex simply cannot and will not go anywhere good.

The *individualization* of sex violates three fundamental biblical principles: worship, relationship, and obedience. The next three chapters will look at sex from the vantage point of these three principles.

SEX IS AN ACT OF WORSHIP

They are two words that may seem strange when placed side by side: sex and worship. It's intuitive to understand these two words as capturing two separate and very different worlds. But worship and sex properly understood cannot be separated. Sex is an act of worship, and the true worship of God will determine what happens in your sexual life. In fact, even the most irreligious person expresses worship every time he engages in some kind of sexual activity, whether mental or physical. Let me say it this way: in sex you are always worshiping something. Your sexual life is shaped by the worship of God, the worship of self, the worship of the other person, or the worship of what you get out of sex. What this means is that in sex you and I are always surrendering our hearts to something. The things we say, do, and seek in sex are all ruled by the desire for something. In this most intimate of human activities, you are always revealing who God designed you to be—a worshiper. You don't put down your worship nature when you're having sex. You and I have worshiped our way through every moment of any kind of sexual activity to which we've given ourselves.

Think for a moment how your sexual life would change if you took the worship nature of your humanity seriously. Think of what a difference it would make if you always connected sex to worship. Think of what would change in your sexual thoughts, desires, choices, and actions. You see, if sex is all about you worshiping you ("I want to rule my life and do what I want to do"), it will never work as God intended. If sex is all about you worshiping your partner ("I can't live without the love of this other person"), sex will never work as God intended. Or if sex is all about worshiping what you get out of sex ("I can't live without what sex does for me"), it will never work as God intended. Worship of anything other than God always ends in the worship of self and the *individualization* of things that are designed by God to connect us to things that are bigger than our wants, needs, and pleasures.

There is a passage in the New Testament that gets to the practical core of what it means to connect sex and worship. It lays out what it means to approach your sexuality as a worshiper of God and what it means to practically acknowledge that, if sex is all about worship, it can't be just about you. Read carefully the words of this passage:

"All things are lawful for me," but not all things are helpful. "All things are lawful for me," but I will not be dominated by anything. "Food is meant for the stomach and the stomach for food"—and God will destroy both one and the other. The body is not meant for sexual immorality, but for the Lord, and the Lord for the body. And God raised the Lord and will also raise us up by his power. Do you not know that your bodies are members of Christ? Shall I then take the members of Christ and make them members of a prostitute? Never! Or do you not know that he who is joined to a prostitute becomes one body with her? For, as it is written, "The two will become one flesh." But he who is joined to the Lord becomes one spirit with him. Flee from sexual immorality. Every other sin a person commits is outside the body, but the sexually immoral person sins against his own body. Or do you not know that your body is a temple of the Holy Spirit within you, whom you have from God? You are not your own, for you were bought with a price. So glorify God in your body. (1 Cor. 6:12–20)

Paul looks at the subject of sex through the lens of four worship principles and two worship commands. Each one of the worship principles points you to your identity as a child of God. (Mastery—I have been designed for worship. Eternity—I have been hardwired for eternity. Unity—grace has made me one with Jesus Christ. Ownership—I am now the property of Christ.) This is as helpful and as practical a discussion of the implications of worship on the most intimate and personal areas of life as you will find in all of Scripture.

I think for years I had an unbiblical view of my own sexuality. I'm not talking about sexual sin in my life. I'm talking about a failure to have a robustly biblical view of this very important part of the human existence. My biblical view of sex was limited to a catalog of things that God said I could not do. It was a boundary view of the Bible and sex. It was as if all the Bible did was define the boundaries that you must stay inside in your sexual life. So I thought that as long as I stayed inside of God's boundaries, sex belonged to me for my pleasure. I think many, many Christians hold this view. They wrongly think that the Bible's relation to sex is regulatory and little else. But this legal understanding of the Bible and sex didn't help or protect me as I thought it would.

You see, the law of God is excellent when it comes to exposing sin. God's law is a wonderful guide for how you were designed to live your life. But the law has no power at all to defeat sin or deliver you from it. The problem with the Bible being viewed as a book of sex boundaries is that you don't then seek or get biblical help for the place where the sexual struggle actually takes place. My problem isn't that I am ignorant of what God says is right or wrong when it comes to sex; my problem is that even in the face of knowing what is right and wrong, I still desire and do things that I shouldn't. My problem is that there are times when I don't care what God says is right or wrong. I want what I want. I will have what I will have. I will use what has been given for whatever purpose I choose. It is this deeper struggle that I need help with. It is because of this deeper struggle that Jesus had to come. You could argue that Jesus came to rescue sex or, maybe more explicitly, in sex to rescue you from you. Paul's discussion roots at this deeper level.

SEX AND FOUR INESCAPABLE WORSHIP PRINCIPLES

1) The Principle of Mastery

The principle of mastery is the principle of principles. It addresses design, struggle, and solution. You simply cannot understand the sexual struggle and how it is solved without understanding this principle. Hear Paul's words again: "'All things are lawful for me,' but not all things are helpful. 'All things are lawful for me,' but I will not be dominated by anything. 'Food is meant for the stomach and the stomach for food'—and God will destroy both one and the other. The body is not meant for sexual immorality, but for the Lord, and the Lord for the body'" (vv. 12–13). Let's unpack the thunderous importance of these little sentences.

When Paul says, "All things are lawful for me," he is not giving his worldview; he is parroting the misconception of people around him. Classic antinomianism would say that because Christ fulfilled the law, I do not have to live its requirements anymore. I am free from the law, bottom line. Yes, I am free from the requirements of the law in terms of earning acceptance with God, but I am not free from the law in terms of its being God's ordained moral claim on my life as his creature. But Paul's answer to this false-gospel worldview is even more forceful and eloquent than a mere critique of this misunderstanding of the work of Christ and God's law. He essentially responds this way: "Even if everything were legal, I would still have a big problem, because when it comes to sex I don't just have a legal problem; I have a mastery problem. Because of my mastery problem, even God's good things become bad things, because they become ruling things. My struggle is deeper than an ignorance or misunderstanding of God's law. My problem is that there are moments when I am a rebel against God's law because I have given over my heart to another master."

Paul is saying, "When it comes to things like sex, my problem is a fickle, wandering, easily disloyal heart. I say that Jesus is my Lord, but I am daily tempted to give my heart over to the rule of other masters." You see, between the already and the not yet, every day is a mastery struggle. Every day in every area of my life a battle of rulers wages in my heart. Every day I am tempted to shift masters. Every day I am tempted to tell myself that it is okay to give my heart to a master other than Jesus for just a few minutes; after all, in the grand scheme of things what difference will it make?

Sex is one in a list of a whole catalog of created things that are good things but can become bad things when they become ruling things. If you allow your heart to be ruled by sex or sexual pleasure or sexual power or whatever other thing sex gets you, you will not only misuse this good gift of God but also end up being controlled by it. Sexual distortion and sexual addiction do not exist because sex itself is bad but because we have put it in a place that God never intended it to be.

So what do we do about this mastery struggle? What do we do about our fickle, wandering hearts? How do we protect ourselves from the insanity of being mastered by something other than the one true Master? Well, let's go back to Paul's words again.

Why does he insert, "'Food is meant for the stomach and the stomach for food'—and God will destroy both one and the other"? Here Paul recites a second popular misconception that essentially says, "It doesn't make any difference what you do with your body because your body and what fills it will all be destroyed anyway."

And as he did with the first misconception, Paul answers this false-gospel worldview with the principle of mastery. What you do with your body right here and right now does matter, because your body has a master—the Lord himself. You can never properly understand the gospel of Jesus Christ and conclude that what you do with your body is your business or what you do with your body doesn't matter. Jesus gives you his grace not to free you to live as though you're king but to live in the freedom of honoring him as your King.

Now what does all this have to do with sex? The answer is, everything. One of the places where I most powerfully and practically reveal what truly rules my heart is in sex. My sex life will be shaped and directed by whatever is my street-level master. And I will only ever stay inside of God's wise boundaries when he is the functional ruler of my heart. Does that discourage you? It does me! Because I don't do very well in keeping God central in my life all the time, every day. I am very skilled at convincing myself that there are things that I deserve or things that I cannot live without. I am very skilled at convincing myself that this little trespass, just this once, isn't such a big deal. I don't know how to keep my heart from being fickle. I don't think I have the power to keep myself safe.

It is here that this first principle preaches the gospel to us. My hope in the struggle for sexual purity or any other victory over sin is not found in my perfect submission to Christ as my master, but in his perfect submission to the will of the Father on my behalf. In my sin, weakness, and struggle I do not have to be paralyzed by fear or hide in shame. I can stand before a holy God, broken as I am, and cry out for his forgiveness, help, protection, and rescue. And I do not have to fear his rejection, because my standing before him is based on the righteousness of the Savior, not on my own righteousness.

But there is something else. The gospel of Jesus Christ also guarantees me help in this struggle of mastery. Jesus is with me, in me, and for me. He fights on my behalf even when I fail to have the sense or the willingness to fight. Now that's hope!

2) The Principle of Eternity

This second worship principle, the principle of eternity, is of equal significance. Hear the words of Paul again: "And God raised the Lord and will also raise us up by his power" (v. 14). Why does Paul interject this little sentence about the resurrection of Jesus and our future resurrection? The answer is that Paul knows himself, and he knows his audience. One of the core issues in the sexual struggle is our tendency to treat a particular moment of life as if it is all there is, all that we have. Permit me to explain.

By God's design you and I are hardwired for eternity. That means that every human being carries around a desire for paradise. So there are only two ways to live. Either you think that this is all there is and therefore take control of your life and relationships and try to turn this moment into the eternity that it will never be, or you understand that this moment isn't your final destination but a preparation for a destination to come.

These are two vastly different ways of living. The first person tells himself that he's only going to go around once, so he'd better get all the pleasure he possible can before death takes him out of the game, and the other person recognizes the brokenness of the world, the temporary and unfulfilling pleasures of the here and now, and looks forward to the eternal joys of the forever that is to come. Eternity amnesia makes a mess out of sex. It puts the focus on present pleasure rather than on eternal joy. It causes us to be driven rather than patient and restful. It diminishes the eternal significance of little decisions, making life more about what we've been able to experience than about how we have lived. It causes us to replace the focus on God's purpose for creating us with a focus on our personal pleasure. It makes us hope for a satisfaction we won't find this side of eternity and to look for it in places it simply cannot be found.

It may sound weird to you, but you and I were meant to have sex (inside of God's boundaries) with eternity in view. We were meant to know that sex will never be the paradise we are searching for. We were meant to understand that sex will never satisfy our hearts. We were meant to understand that a particular moment is more about the hardship of preparation than about the quest for personal pleasure. Our sexual lives were meant to be protected by the long view of life. Living with eternity in view is one of the things God uses to direct and purify our sexual existence. Between the already and the not yet, it is far better for our sexual life to be lived on the basis of restful hope (the best is yet to come) than on fearful hunger (this is all we have; we'd better get all we can).

If you're God's child, the resurrection of Jesus guarantees you a future way beyond the glory of any pleasures you will experience in this right-here, right-now broken world. Again, Jesus lived with eternity in view in every way, and he did this on your behalf and for your benefit so that you would have the grace you need to live for something bigger than the temporary pleasures of the here and now, including sex.

3) The Principle of Unity

Here, in the principle of unity, Paul reminds us with one of the most precious mysteries of the gospel. Hear his words: "Do you not know that your bodies are members of Christ? Shall I then take the members of Christ and make them members of a prostitute? Never! Or do you not know that he who is joined to a prostitute becomes one body with her? For, as it is written, 'The two will become one flesh.' But he who is joined to the Lord becomes one spirit with him. Flee from sexual immorality. Every other sin a person commits is outside the body, but the sexually immoral person sins against his own body" (vv. 15–18). With language that is shocking and sobering, Paul reminds us of something that we must always remember as we deal with the relationships, pleasures, and temptations of this here-and-now fallen world. If you are God's child, you have been united with Christ. This is not just an amorphous spiritual reality but a physical one as well. All of what makes you *you* has been united to Christ. Your emotionality, your physicality, your mentality, your personality, your psychology, and your spirituality have all been united to Christ.

This means that you take Christ with you wherever you are and whatever you are doing. Union with Christ means your life isn't bifurcated. You don't have Christ and the spiritual part of your life alongside of everything else. He *is your life.* It's Christ in and with you in the most intimate, secret, and, yes, even dark moments of your life. He is united to every thought and desire. He is connected to every fantasy and choice. He is there during every action and reaction.

So Paul asks the key question, "Shall I then take the members of Christ [the parts of my body] and make them members of a prostitute?" (v. 15). What a perspective on sexual sin. It is much, much more than a breaking of some ancient abstract law that God decided to lay on us. No, for me as a believer sexual sin is a horrific violation of my relationship with Christ. It is loving my pleasure so deeply that I am willing to connect the Holy One to what is unholy. Paul is describing an unthinkable act of selfishness, disloyalty, and rebellion. Since I am one with Christ and since sex creates a one-flesh bond with a prostitute, I am essentially in my selfishness willing to unite Christ to a prostitute. No wonder Paul says, "Never!" (v. 15).

I am deeply persuaded that there are few things more protective and purifying to keep in mind as you deal with sexual desire and sexual temptation than the reality and totality of your union with your Savior. Jesus Christ is in you and you in him, even in the most secret and holy moments of your sexual life. And he is with you as well in the secret and most unholy moments.

Does this make you afraid? Ashamed? Guilty? Paralyzed? This beautiful union with Christ, which only grace could create, also guarantees you all the grace you need to live within that reality. It guarantees all the grace you need to wage war with your desires. It gives all the grace you need to say no to what is unholy and yes to what is pleasing in the eyes of him to whom you are united. And it offers you the forgiveness that you will need as you fail once again. Here is your hope: when Christ unites himself to you, he doesn't leave his grace at the door. He brings to this union all of those provisions of grace that you and I need to be what we're supposed to be and to do what we're supposed to do, in sex and in everything else. Your union with Christ welcomes you to be a *sober celebrant*. Sober, because you have grasped the seriousness of your union with Christ, and a celebrant, because you understand the hope and help this union provides that can be found no other way.

4) The Principle of Ownership

Here is Paul's capstone principle, the principle of ownership. "Or do you not know that your body is a temple of the Holy Spirit within you, whom you have from God? You are not your own, for you were bought with a price" (vv. 19–20). First, Paul wants every believer to know that grace has claimed your body for a higher purpose than personal, physical pleasure. Your body has been chosen for the higher purpose than anything you could have ever planned or even had the ability to imagine. God Almighty, in the power and glory of his Spirit, has moved in! Now remember, Paul is reminding you of this in the context of a discussion of the gospel/worship implications on your sexuality. As a believer, whatever you do in your sex life you do as the temple of the Most High God! Wow! Could there be a more sobering identity concept for the believer to grasp and live out?

The next thing Paul wants you to consider is that this means the temple that is your body does not belong to you anymore. A new landlord has moved in and has taken over the management of the building. He has claimed the building for his purposes. No longer a personal pleasure place, the building that is your body has been claimed as a temple for the worship of God alone, and everything you do and all the ways that you do it must be done with this new purpose in mind.

Finally, so that in the midst of daily temptation from inside and outside, you would take all of this seriously, Paul reminds you of what it cost God to claim you as your own and grace you to be part of something far better than you would have chosen for yourself. The heavy price was the death of his Son. What an insult in the face of that price to act as if you have the right to do whatever you want with your body, whenever you want to do it, and with whomever.

Again, does this high calling defeat and discourage you? Know that what God calls you to, your Savior has already done on your behalf so that in your failure you can run to God and not from him. Your standing with God is never based on the degree of the purity of your heart and hands but on the perfect life of Christ lived for your sake. Confess the places in your sexual life where you think or act as though you own you, and cry out for the forgiving and transforming grace that is yours because your Savior was willing to pay the price.

These four principles are worldview game changers. *Mastery*—your sex life will be shape by who or what rules your heart. *Eternity*—your sex life will be shaped by whether you live for the temporary pleasures of the here and now or with eternity in view. *Unity*—your sex life will be shaped either by bifurcating your life into the spiritual and secular or by acknowledging that all that makes up you has been united to Christ, and you take Christ wherever you go. *Ownership*—your sex life will be shaped either by acting as if your body belongs to you or by acknowledging that it has been purchased by God for his higher purpose. And your sex life will be shaped either by forgetting the gospel of Jesus Christ that is preached by each of these principles and hiding in guilt, shame, and fear, or by remembering that Jesus perfectly did all of these things so that you, in weakness and failure, would be welcomed into God's presence and receive all the forgiving, transforming, and empowering grace you need to progressively live sexually pure in a world that has gone sexually insane.

SEX AND TWO INESCAPABLE WORSHIP COMMANDS

Now standing on the foundation of the four sex-and-worship principles that we have just examined, Paul leaves us with two simple commands. One is defensive and protective; the other is positive and missional. It is important to note that neither command makes any sense without the worship principles upon which each stands. Each command tells you practically how to live out the personal sexual implications of the identity/worldview that the four principles delineate. This passage really does have an *indicative* then *imperative* structure. Paul starts by saying, "This is who you are because this is what God has done (the four sex-and-worship principles), so now this is how to live in light of what God has done (the two sex-and-worship commands)."

I cannot adequately express how much I wish I had been exposed to the practical, moral wisdom of this passage as a young man, and I cannot tell how sad I am presently that this passage isn't taught with more regularity and clarity wherever God's Word is taken seriously.

1) The command to flee sexual immorality.

Here's the bottom line of this defensive and protective command: if you are going to live in the sexual domain of your life in the way that God has called you to live in the middle of this world that has gone sexually insane, you are going to have to be willing to do a whole lot of running. You have to be willing to run from thoughts that work to paint as beautiful what God has forbidden. You are going to have to run from desires that at times seem too powerful to resist. You are going to have to run from the seductive whisper of the enemy who will lure you with lies. You are going to have to run from situations and locations that play to your weaknesses. You are going to have to run from pride that tells you that you are stronger than you really are. You are going to have to run from selfishness that would allow you to use others for your own pleasure. You are going to have to run from things you would love to participate in but expose you to things you cannot handle. You are simply going to have to run from anything, anywhere, and from any person that is immoral in the eyes of your Savior. You have to be willing to run.

Paul is not calling us to medieval monasticism. We know that the greatest sexual danger to each of us exists inside of us, not outside of us. We know that running won't make us morally pure. But running acknowledges the presence and power of the sin that still lives inside us and how it makes us susceptible to temptation and sadly able to see as beautiful and beneficial what God calls ugly and dangerous. As you work to separate yourself from what God names as immoral, you cry out to God to do what you cannot do, that is, to deliver you from you. God calls you to do what he has empowered you by grace to do, as he does for you what you cannot do for yourself. How amazing his grace is!

The question for you is, where in your sexual life do you need to do a better job of running from what God has called and empowered you to run from?

2) The command to glorify God in your body.

Paul ends with the call to live for something bigger than you. You have been chosen by God's sovereign grace to live for his glory. Even in the most secret recesses of your private thoughts and desires, you have been chosen to live for his glory. Even in the most naked, private, and intimate activities of your body, you have been chosen to live for his glory. Even in those moments of the most powerful physical and emotional fulfillment, you have been chosen to live for his glory. Even in the most amazing moments of relational connectivity, you have been chosen to live for his glory. Grace has sanctified your whole life, all that makes up you. Grace has set it apart for a greater, higher purpose. Grace has given you new identity, potential, and dignity. Grace has lifted you out of the self-centered mire of the "me-ism" of sin that gives you little purpose greater than the fulfillment of the moment, so that you can live with greater meaning and purpose than you have ever lived with before. Grace gives you back your sanity and your humanity. Grace connects you once again to the purpose for which you were designed and given breath. Grace rescues you from your bondage to passions run wild and thoughts run amuck to live in the sanity of God-consciousness that colors your every thought, desire, choice, word, and action. And in so doing, grace introduces you to the highest and most fulfilling pleasures that a human being could ever experience. You see, your greatest pleasures and joys are only ever found in living as you were designed to live, that is, for him.

If sex is about worship, it can't be just about you. "Just about me" sex is sex gone insane. Sex for the glory of the Creator is sex made sane again. Sex as an act of the worship of God is sex made right again. And in this struggle of glory and worship, God meets us with his tender and patient grace. He invites us to confess, believe, and follow and empowers us in every way to live inside of his gracious invitation. So, how are you doing?

7

IF SEX IS ABOUT RELATIONSHIP, THEN IT CAN'T BE JUST ABOUT YOU

He had little desire or motivation at all. If honest, he would have told you that he found her irritating in many ways. He had managed to forge out a schedule and a set of relational rules that meant he could be married but pretty much live on his own, even though they were in the same house. He did all he could to tolerate a civil back-and-forth between them at the dinner table, but he found most of what she talked about to be incredibly boring. He didn't like her friends and tried to excuse himself from as many of her activities as he could get away with. He controlled their finances and their purchases and had the only voice as to how the family was run. He worked hard and provided well, but beyond that, there was little that was loving in his relationship with his wife.

But despite all the distance and disregard, there was one way he demanded that they connect every day, which was to have sex every evening before sleep. He said it was both his right and God's will. Night after night they had unrelational, unloving sex. Night after night she did what she was told, even if it was uncomfortable or embarrassing to her. Night after night he would go to sleep sexually satisfied, and she would go to sleep sad and confused and feeling powerless. Night after night she hoped he would fall asleep before demanding sex or just give her one night's break, but it never happened. After giving herself in the most intimate of human activities, the next morning he would dress and get ready to go without even acknowledging her existence. Day after day she would dread his coming home because she knew the cycle would begin all over again.

So, what is your response to the sex life of this couple? What would you say to this man? What would you say to his wife? How close is their sexual life to God's intention?

SEX IS INESCAPABLY RELATIONAL

There is something deeply disturbing about the sex life of this couple: it isn't really the sex life of the couple; it is the sex life of the man forced upon the woman. At a profound level, though this couple is married, their sex life is a violation of what God designed sex to be. Their sex life is yet another example of the *individualization* of sex. Sex for this man is not an act of love. It is not an act of the worship of God; it is a lifestyle of the pursuit of personal pleasure at the expense of the service of and dignity of his wife.

Sex by God's design is meant to occur in the context of two communities of love. Love for God and neighbor is the only location where sex can live according to God's plan. Let me give you the bottom line of this chapter right now: *a living commitment to community protects sex and purifies it from the sin of individualization.* In other words, sex only lives with beauty and health when it grows out of the soil of the two great commands. God, who is himself a community, ordained sex to be an act of community, and when it isn't, it loses its shelter from danger and destruction. Sex outside of community cannot work as God intended and becomes another example of the insanity that results from the selfishness of sin. You can't just be committed to having sex; you need also to be committed to the only context in which this thing that you desire was created for. Let's examine the "commitment to community" context in which God-honoring sex must live.

SEX AND LOVING GOD

This may sound a bit weird, but it is true nonetheless: one of the principal ways human beings love God is in their sexual life. Since you and I were created to be sexual beings, with sexual desire and physical sexual organs, dealing with sex in some way is inescapable. And since we're created to love God above everything else that exists in the world he created, dealing with God in some way is also inescapable. So it is impossible for these two things not to come together in your life. You will express your sexuality in some way, and you will relate to God in some way. If you are acknowledging that there is no higher, holier call in all your life than loving God, then you will want everything in your sexual life to be an expression of that love.

Sex is dangerous when it is only motivated by love of you. Sex is dangerous when it is only motivated by love for the other person. Sex is dangerous when it is only motivated by love for pleasure. Sex is dangerous when it is only motivated by love for comfort. Sex is dangerous when it is only motivated by love for control. Sex is dangerous when it is only motivated by love for sex. Sex is only ever purified and protected when what motivates us in thought, desire, and action is a living, submissive, joyful, willing, street-level love for God. Sexual sin always has a lack of love for God at its core. Or, in other words, in illicit sex we are replacing the love we should have for God with love for something else.

You see, it is always my relationship with God (or lack of it) that will shape and determine my relationship with you. If I love God as I should, I will want to relate to you in ways that please and honor him. My love for him will mean that his pleasure trumps my pleasure. It will mean that I have a greater joy in doing his will than in getting my own way. And there will be a joy and a willingness to all of this. Perhaps the core character quality of true love is willingness. Love loves to love. Love doesn't see love as a burden or a hassle. Love doesn't love begrudgingly. Love doesn't love kicking and screaming. Love doesn't look for ways of avoiding the call to love. Love doesn't search for ways of escape. Love isn't two-faced and devious. Love is willing and ready to love.

Jesus said it this way: "If you love me, you will keep my commandments" (John 14:15). There is the willingness. Jesus is saying, "If you love me, then you will not see my commands as burdensome. You will not chafe against them. You will willingly and joyfully do what I have told you to do." For most of us, this is very humbling because it requires us to admit what we don't really want to have to admit. When we are involved in sexual sin (sex outside of God's clear boundaries), we have done what we've done because we do not love God as we should. And when God is not in his rightful place, we invariably put ourselves in his position, and we make it all about us. At that point we become self-sovereigns who seek to rule the world for our own pleasure and take as our possession things that do not belong to us.

Let me give you two examples. Think first of the woman who is lying in bed early in the morning fantasizing about sex with someone other than her husband. Consider the godlike posture of her fantasy. She is unhappy with the world that actually exists because she did not create it and she does not control it, so the real world does not do her biding or give her what she wants. So in her bed on this morning, she seeks to raise herself to the throne of God and in her mind creates a world as she wants it to be and then rules that world as its absolute sovereign. Everything in her self-created world is her possession, and everything in her world submits to her pleasure. This world is attractive to her because in it she is creator, lord, and king. So she sets the rules. She uses what she has created as she wants to use it and for whatever pleasure she seeks. And she'll visit this world again because it is way more attractive to her than the world that really exists, which has been created by and is ruled by someone other than her.

The man she has taken for her pleasure in her fantasy does not belong to her, and the things she has dreamed of doing with him are not her right to do. She has removed God from her universe, taken his throne, possessed what belongs to him, thrown away his rules, and written a new set. The whole thing is an outrageous violation on the loving community that she was created to have with God that would then shape every thought, desire, choice, and action in her life. Her problem isn't first that she loves herself too much or fails to love the man that she has objectified in her fantasy. The problem is even greater than a failure to love God. It is really more serious than that. In her fantasy, even if just for a moment, she has killed God, taken his position, recreated the world as a garden for her own pleasure, and used it as she and she alone wills. What she is doing in her bed is not a little thing. It is a horrible thing, and each time she does it, it will make it harder for her to accept the real world where she doesn't have the position of God. In the real world she will be more and more tempted to act as the sovereign that she isn't and to attempt to possess and experience what does not belong to her. Her fantasy is the portal to greater sexual insanity, but she doesn't know it. In fact, she prides herself in not acting upon the dreams she has been able to conjure up.

Something beautiful, purifying, and protective is missing in her heart. It is something that God intended to be the core motivator of every person he created. What is it? It is willing, joyful, submissive, and active rubber-meets-the-road love for him. It is the only place where sexual purity is to be found. Sexual purity begins in the heart with a love for God that overwhelms all the other loves that battle for the allegiance of the heart.

Or consider this second example. A man is walking home from work and lusting after the woman approaching him on the sidewalk. He slows down his walk to get a longer look, and he turns around and watches as she passes by him. Think with me again about the godlike posture of the man in this encounter. First, he is treating this moment as if it belongs to him. It's as if he is sovereign and she is on the sidewalk according to his will and for his pleasure. He is owning this moment as his own. This location is his location, there to bring him the pleasure that is his right. He's the self-appointed deity of the moment. He thinks of no other God and worships no one but himself. The world has shrunk to the size of his desire, and he rules it for his pleasure. He doesn't give a rip at that moment about what is right or wrong because there is for that moment no higher authority than himself. He will have what he will have, even if it is only the right to stare at body parts and imagine having them for his pleasure.

But there is more. For that moment he is stealing God's creation from him and taking it as his own. He has no right to this woman. She does not actually belong to him in any way, but he takes her with his eyes and his mind. He tries to slow down the moment in order to enjoy his sexual thievery for as long as he can. He's ripped this woman out of the hands of God and claimed her as his own for whatever momentary pleasure he can achieve. She feels his eyes and is uncomfortable. She wants to get away, but she has to walk by. She feels a bit violated, but it's not the first time. She's walked by this guy and other guys like him before.

In that moment this man is the fool. He has denied God's existence. He has set himself up as God. He has robbed God of his creation. He has thrown God off his throne. He has a much deeper problem than his wandering eyes and his fickle affections. He has become comfortable with dethroning God and possessing what does not belong to him, and if he continues to do it with his mind, he will begin to do it with his hands. Remember, lust does not lust for more lust. Lust lusts for the actual thing, the real experience. He is in danger because his heart has become comfortable with what by God's design is a horrible, unnatural thing—a life-shaping, danger-exposing lack of love for God.

It is recognition of and living for the community with God for which I was created that keeps my sexual life pure. There is simply no other way. It is heart-controlling love for God that protects my heart from wandering to all the places it could wander in this world that has gone sexually insane.

As you read this, what are you thinking? I'll tell you what I have been thinking. I have had to face the sad truth that I dethrone God all the time. I view the world as mine again and again. It is the tragedy of remaining sin. There are ways in which I still want God's throne and desire to want as mine what belongs to him. Perhaps it is in a moment of lust on the street, or an impatient word to someone who's made me wait, or envying what someone else has. As I have written, I have been forced to acknowledge that I am not free from the struggles about which I am writing. I am still capable of being that God-denying fool. It is to my grief that I must confess that there are times when I think I am smarter than God, that my rule would be better than his. It is to my grief that I must face the fact that this never, ever leads anywhere good.

Does this mean that I am without hope? How could it be, with all I know and all I've experienced as God's child, that these struggles still exist? Sure, there are times when I get it right and my heart is filled with love and gratitude for God, but not always. In the face of the acknowledgment of my fickle heart, my hope still remains firm and secure. Why? Because my security has never been in the degree of my love for God but in the unshakable and eternal character of his love for me. And as I come to him in poverty of spirit, not only will he not turn me away; he will greet me with open arms and the lavish provision of his right-here, right-now grace. His transforming love remains faithful even when mine doesn't. He will not abandon the promises of his grace, even when I don't value them as I should. He will not quit being my Lord in those moments when I would rather be my own lord. He will not fold up his kingdom and go home when I would rather construct a kingdom of my own that does my bidding. Yes, he will chasten me with his hands of fatherly grace, but he will not throw me out of his family and abandon the work in me and for me that he has begun.

So I run to him and confess that sex isn't my problem; vertical love is. I confess that sex is where my ongoing temptation to dethrone God is revealed, controls my world, and writes my own rules for my selfish purpose and pleasure. Again, I kneel before him, confessing the disloyalty of my heart, seeking the grace that is my only hope of purity of heart and hands. I pray again that he would give me the heart to love willingly and consistently until the struggle to love is no more. And I pray that this living and active love for him would overwhelm any love I have for something in the creation that battles for the affection of my heart.

These prayers are significant because the struggle for sexual purity is really a struggle to keep God in his rightful place in your heart—at the center of your affections and motivations.

SEX AND LOVING YOUR NEIGHBOR

Sex is also purified and protected by a second community of love, love for your neighbor. Illicit sex never treats another as an object of affection. Illicit sex is never motivated and shaped by self-sacrificing love for another. Illicit sex never wants what is good for another. Illicit sex doesn't willingly submit to another's needs. Illicit sex doesn't answer the higher call to be part of what God is doing in another's life. Illicit sex always replaces relational love with entitled, demanding, selfish, personal pleasure. Illicit sex is all about me to the detriment of you. Illicit sex objectifies and dehumanizes another. You become to me less than God's image bearer. You are reduced to little more than an object for my momentary sexual pleasure. Illicit sex denies the second Great Commandment, uproots sex from its God-intended community, and plants it in the world of individual pleasure, where it was never meant to germinate and grow.

One of the horrific things about pornography is the way in which it is fundamentally anti-relational. Sex is reduced to graphic fantasies, sexual activities, and sexual climax. There is not even a consideration of relationship, let alone committed marital love. The man and the woman are together not as an expression of anything remotely relational but because they want sexual pleasure. So rather than expressing affection of any kind, the sex they are having is just a personal pursuit of sex. The man uses the body of the woman for sex, and the woman uses the body of the man for sex. Its sex for sex's sake or sex for money's sake, but it is not sex for love's sake, because there is no love needed when all you are trying to do is use the body of the other to reach physical sexual climax. Pornographic videos tend not to be love stories.

One of the horrible things about sex in advertising is that it is fundamentally anti-relational. The body of a woman is used to sell an automobile, for instance. Now think about this. The advertiser is intentionally playing to the sexual desires of male consumers, using the sexuality of the woman to attract the attention of the potential buyer. He is trying to create a connection between the sexiness of the woman and the "sexiness" of the car. He doesn't care if the man buys the car as a "sex" decision rather than as a sound financial decision as long as he buys the car. The woman in the ad is reduced to something less than human. She is not respected for her mind, her character, and her gifts. She is not esteemed and loved. It is her sexuality that you notice, her body that you desire. Sadly, in the ad, the woman, who is made in the image of God, is reduced to the level of the car—a sexy object designed to bring you pleasure. The intentionality and methodology of the commercial is a denial of the Second Great Commandment. Illicit sex always denies this command because it is not interested in relationship. It's only interested in personal sexual pleasure.

God's design is that sex would only ever take place in the context of a committed, life-long relationship between a man and a woman in marriage. Sex is protected and purified by this commitment to tender, faithful, self-sacrificing, other-serving love. In this context I am not after my own pleasure and using you to get it. In this context, even in my most intimate, physical, and exciting connection to you, I am loving you and looking out for your welfare. The way I relate to you and touch you and the things we do in sex are all then guided and directed by relational love, not just sexual excitement.

Now, I think this helps us understand why there is so much sexual dysfunction even in the lives of married couples. I am convinced that usually the problem isn't that couples are ignorant of the structure and function of their bodies. As I've written before, I don't think we need a bunch of new Christian "body part" books. Look, most of us know where stuff is on the body, and we know how things were made to function. Little of this dysfunction is the result of ignorance.

Here's what the problem is: you will always drag the character and quality of your marriage relationship into the marriage bed because sex is fundamentally relational. To deny that sex is a relationship is just insanity. If I have nourished you and cherished you, if I have been willing to serve you, if I have been giving, forgiving, forbearing, kind, gentle, patient, and respectful of you in our everyday relationship, then in this moment where there is no protection, where you are literally naked next to me in the most vulnerable of human moments, you will know that you can trust me to love you, and you can relax, naked in my arms. But if I have been critical, entitled, and demanding, if I have been unforgiving and bitter, if I have been impatient, rude, selfish and unkind, in this moment where you are naked next to me, you will not feel safe. You will fear that what you have experienced with me apart from sex, you will now experience in sex. You will be afraid that you will be used and criticized rather than loved and nurtured. And because you are afraid, you find it hard to give yourself in the way you must in order for sex to work as God intended.

Most sexually dysfunctional couples don't need sex education as much as they need relational confession and reconciliation. Because God designed sex to be experienced in the context of relationship and as an expression of that relationship, you can't escape the nature of your relationship to your husband or wife when you are having sex. It simply isn't possible. What these dysfunctional couples are trying to do is find sexual pleasure outside of a commitment to the kind of relationship that God has called them to have. And even though they are having sex in marriage, they have little commitment to the relationship of love that is meant to be the context for this intimate act, and therefore, at the level of their hearts, they are in violation of God's plan. Unloving, demanding sex that is not in the context of living, active, relational love simply isn't God-honoring sex.

Let me take this discussion further. I understand why so many men struggle with Internet pornography. If sex for you has not been an act of relational love, if what you have essentially done is use the body of your wife for your own selfish sexual pleasure, if your wife has been reduced to a means of you getting off, then it makes sense that you would be very tempted to replace her with digital images and selfish fantasies that accomplish the same thing. There are marriages in which men are sexually unkind to their wife, sexually demanding, sexually selfish, and sexually critical. They are much more interested in their wife's sexually performing for them then they are committed to loving their wife sexually. They have little interest in the comfort and pleasure of their wives. They demand things that make their wife uncomfortable and instill guilt in the face of their wife's protests. The sex they have in their marriages doesn't look like love. It looks like the self-sovereign, my-pleasure-first individualization of sex that is everywhere in the surrounding culture. Shockingly, they use the wife's marriage vows as a tool to get her to submit to whatever selfish sexual demands they make, all the while claiming that it is their right. Perhaps without understanding what they are doing, they have denigrated marital sex, bringing it down to a level just above masturbation, and they have reduced their wife to a machine for their own pleasure. This kind of sex life meets none of the requirements to love God or to love neighbor and is therefore horrible in the eyes of God.

Because the sex life of these men in marriage has been more masturbatory than relational, it makes sense that they have little defense against the readily available pornography that offers them the selfish pleasure they seek without the burden of having to relate to another in the process. They easily matriculate from one kind of anti-relational sex to another with none of the love commitments of heart that would protect them and reveal pornography as the horror that it actually is. It is sad that so much of this is going on in the church and maybe even sadder that no one is talking about it.

Sex in marriage isn't made holy simply because it's in marriage, anymore than talk in marriage is made holy because it's in marriage. Both sex and talk are made holy by the intentions of your heart, and the intentions are holy when by powerful transforming grace you love God above all else and love your neighbor as yourself.

Part of the insanity of human culture when it comes to sex is our ability to philosophically or practically deny its God-ordained relational context. You can do this inside or outside of marriage. Yes, according to God's design only married couples are free to have sex, but just because you're married, it doesn't necessarily follow that your sex life is an expression of the two Great Commandments. If it isn't, it is neither honoring to God nor treating your neighbor as God commands.

And why do we fail to have sex that is an active expression of biblical love for one another? We do so because we fail to love

God as we should, inserting ourselves in God's position, making it all about us and using the body of another for our selfish pleasure. Divine dethronement is at the root of sexual insanity of every kind. If you are questing for the position of God, you will not behave as you should in any area of your life.

And for this insanity Jesus willingly went to the cross, so that "those who live would no longer live for themselves" (2 Cor. 5:15), no longer for divine dethronement. Jesus died to dethrone you and to enthrone God in your heart. Now in that there is hope, not only for your sex life, but for everything else in your life as well.

8

IF SEX IS ABOUT OBEDIENCE, THEN IT CAN'T BE JUST ABOUT YOU

I tell parents all the time that one of the first and most important heart issues for young children is the issue of authority. Sinners tend to like authority. They tend to want to be their own authority. Sinners are oriented to self-sovereignty and the writing of their own moral code. Children tend not to ask their parents for more rules and closer accountability. Children tend not to celebrate when they have been told what to do. Children tend to look at authority as something that robs them of freedom. Children don't tend to love authority and see it as a blessing. Natural rebellion to authority, which in some way is the state of all sinners, is one of the principal heart struggles for everyone who has ever lived.

Why is all this important? It's important because you will never deal with the sex issue until you have first dealt with the authority issue. The sexual struggle and the sexual insanity of the culture are rooted in something deeper than sex. They are rooted in a rejection of the authority of God over every area of human existence. They are rooted in a deep desire for self-rule. They are rooted in the drive that people have to take charge of their own lives and do what they want with them. They are rooted in the deep and abiding cultural heresy that says, "My body belongs to me and no one has the right to tell me what to do with it." The sexual insanity that is all around us is, in fact, anti-authority madness that cannot and will not go anywhere good because it violates the very nature of who we are and how the world was designed to operate.

You see, little children, grown men, and women alike need to be confronted with the stark reality that it will never be about them because they have been born into a world that by its very nature is the celebration of another. They have been born into a world that is not owned by them. They have been born into a world that was not intended to be ruled by them. Any authority humans have is representative or ambassadorial. Human authority is never ultimate. Every human authority is placed where it has been placed to visibly represent the invisible authority of God. Here is the bottom line that must then shape the way you view everything, including sex: the world we live in is a world under rule. This means that I do not have the right to do whatever I want to do, whenever, however, and with whomever I want to do it. Because there is an authority over all things, there is law. And because there is law, for every area of my life there are things that are morally right to do and things that are morally wrong.

So the issue for every human being is, will I submit to the directives of the One who rules over all things, or will I deny his authority and write my own rules? This is the ultimate and inescapable human decision. So sex can't be just about reaching the highest moment of pleasure, because that is an essentially lawless way of looking at sex. Sex has to be about obedience to the law. If there is an authority who rules every dimension of your life, then sex can't be just about you. It is always about his will, his way, his plan, his pleasure, and his glory and about the degree of your willingness to submit to him.

Now, this cuts cross-grain against two foundational lies that somehow, someway, all sinners tend to buy into. The first lie is the lie of autonomy. Here I choose to believe that my life belongs to me so I have the right to invest it any way I want. This would mean that my body belongs to me and I have the right to do with it what I want, which would mean my sexual self belongs to me and I have the right to satisfy it anyway I want. As I have argued before, the doctrine of creation blows this away. Since God created all things, he owns all things. This means there is simply no such condition as human autonomy. Every human being is owned by the One who created him or her, and the Creator alone has the right to say how what he has created is to be used.

The second lie is the lie of self-sufficiency. This tells me that I have everything I need inside of me to be what I'm supposed to be and to do what I'm supposed to do. I do not need the help, wisdom, and guidance of another. I am able to figure it all out, and I am able to live the kind of life I was designed to live with no outside assistance. The fact is really the opposite. Human beings were not created to live independently or self-sufficiently. Human beings were created to be dependent. We were created with fundamental needs that we cannot meet on our own. We are born with a need for wisdom that we don't have. We are born with a need for strength that we do not possess. We all need to be taught and enabled and, because of sin, rescued and transformed as well. The self-made person is a fantasy. The independent human being is a delusion. We are weak and needy, all of us. There simply is no escaping it.

So this is the way that I should view myself, including my sexual self. In sex I will either accept the fact that I am weak and needy and seek the help of my Creator or deny the empirical evidence that I daily give of who I am and act as if I know what I do not know and am able to do what I cannot do. So armed with a belief that my body is my right to use as I choose and that I am wise and strong, I will write my own sex manual and do what I want with my body and the bodies of others, all the while telling myself that I am wise and that what I am doing is good. And day after day I will deny my sexual insanity and blame the trouble that results on others.

It bears repeating that the sexual mess that is all around us is much, much more than a sex mess. It is a mess of self-worship, denial of community, a rejection of authority, and the individualization of sex that results. You cannot move toward sexual sanity without addressing these root issues. You can't isolate sex and successfully fix sex without dealing with the underlying issues that have caused the mess to be the mess that it is.

The little child, who becomes comfortable with rejecting the authority of God as it comes through the authority of his parents, is heading for sexual insanity. The teenage girl who mocks her parents as being hyper-conservative and embarrassingly old-fashioned and so rejects their authority is heading for sexual insanity. The college graduate who has been persuaded that his life is his for the using is headed for sexual insanity. The middle-aged man who thinks he has the independent strength to keep his sexual desires in check is headed for sexual insanity. There is no escaping it; your sex life will always reveal how you are dealing with the unavoidable issue of authority. You submit to the laws of the King, or you set yourself up as king. That's it; there is no neutral world to live in.

WHAT DOES OBEDIENCE LOOK LIKE?

Obedience is more than a set of behaviors; obedience is an attitude of the heart. I will pirate the definition my brother, Tedd, has given for obedience: *Obedience is the willing submission of my heart to God that causes me to do what God has commanded without challenge, excuse, or delay.* May I say at the get-go that an obedient heart will protect and purify your sex life. At the core of sexual purity lives a willing recognition of and submission to the authority of God.

Let's unpack Tedd's definition. The heart of obedience is not doing the right stuff. Rather, the heart of obedience is the heart, and what must live in the heart of the obedient person is a willing submission to God's authority. Obedience that is not willingly submissive is not obedience. If you must force, cajole, threaten, or guilt others into obedience, you have to do that precisely because they are not obedient. They are lacking the willingness that is at the center of every obedient life. Sexually pure people are sexually pure because they have a willing heart, and because they have a willing heart they are ready to say no to powerful desires, raging emotions, and seductive temptations, turning and doing what God has called them to do. The person who fights what is right, who constantly questions it, who looks for ways around it, and who occasionally even mocks it will not be sexually pure for very long because he does not carry around with him an obedient heart. He will not be able to stand against the daily temptations he will face in this world gone sexually insane, and he will not say no to his quickly wandering desires.

This willingness of heart causes me to have a "what-has-God-commanded?" way of looking at my life. I don't mean I live a legalistic, rules-bound existence or that I live tentatively and fearfully. What I am saying is that I have a *boundaries* way of thinking about life. If God is in charge, and if he has decided what is morally right and wrong, and if he has clearly communicated that to me, then there are moral boundaries of heart and behavior inside of which I am called to live. Inside of those boundaries is a life of beautiful freedom and happiness. Outside of those boundaries are danger, destruction, and death.

Think of the word picture of boundaries. Pretend that there is a yard you are living in that contains every good, true, and beautiful thing a human being could ever want, and around the yard is a twenty-foot-high chain-link fence. And consider further that outside, on the other side of the fence, is a world of real danger, things that will cause your death. If you accepted that what is inside the yard is really very good, things that give you life, and if you accepted that what is outside the fence is really very bad, things that lead to death, wouldn't you be thankful for the fence? And wouldn't you be willing to live inside the fence with contentment and joy?

But think with me: if you looked at that fence every day, thinking about how you could get through it or over it, if you touched it or shook it to test its strength, if you tried your best to look through it until you had fence marks on your face, wouldn't you be doing all that because you believe that the good stuff may be on the other side of the fence? You see, you have much more than a behavior problem; you have a boundary problem. You don't believe that the fence is there to ensure you have what is good. No, you have come to believe that the fence is in the way of what is good, and the minute you allow yourself to believe that, you are on your way to finding a means of getting to the other side of the fence.

You see, in my sexual life I am willing to submit to God's commands because, deep within my heart, I really do think they are good. I really do believe that God's laws give life and freedom; they don't rob me of it. I really do believe that God is wise, good, and trustworthy. I really do think that because he is, it is best to live inside his boundaries. So I willingly, in my heart and with my hands, do what God has commanded me to do with my sexual self. I'm not staring at the fence wondering if the good sexual stuff lives out there. I am not haunted by the thoughts of what I am missing. I am not unhealthily curious about the lives and sexual exploits of people on the other side of the fence. And I don't feel disadvantaged because I've been chosen to lives inside the fence. Rather, I turn my back to the fence and joyfully celebrate all the rich and good things I've been given that I would never have had the sense to choose for myself. I wake up each morning not feeling restricted but feeling blessed, and I surely don't equate freedom with having my own way. I know I need fences in every area of my life, including sex, and I know that without God's boundaries I would wander into dangers that would be my doom.

God's boundaries do not inhibit a joyful sexual life; they are the only context in which it can be fully experienced.

Now, back to our definition. The qualifiers in the definition are important: "without challenge." If in my heart I am yelling at God because he won't allow me to do what I want to do, if I am questioning whether he is good and kind, if I am mad because I can't do what others seem free to do, I do not have an obedient heart. The heart of an obedient person doesn't do what is right and kick and scream all the way. Obedient people are not angry with God as they are obeying. You're not actually submissive to God in your sexual life if you're mad at him for what he has told you not to do. You're not obedient to God in sex if you're questioning God's character and his wisdom. You don't have an obedient heart in your sex life if you often wish that the world was ruled by someone else who would give you more freedom. Sexual purity begins with resting assured that what God commands is kind, wise, and good; no need for challenge.

The second qualifier is equally important: "without excuse." An obedient person doesn't excuse his sexual sin; he mourns it. We are never more creative than when we are manufacturing "logical" reasons for stepping beyond God's loving, protective and clear boundaries. We don't want to face the fact that at some point we are all fools and rebels. We want to think of ourselves as wise, reasonable, and moral. So we work to convince ourselves, others, and maybe even God that what we have done is not so bad after all, because look at what we were dealing with or facing. We may even try to convince ourselves that there was no other way, that what looked foolish was really smart, or that it's not so bad just this once. If you can convince yourself that it's right, even good, to live on the other side of God's boundaries, you're heading for sexual insanity of some kind. You will hop God's fences and do with your body and the body of another what you should not do, all the while convincing yourself that it is okay.

The third qualifier is even more deceptive: "without delay."

The obedient heart is quickly willing. If you are willingly submitting to God, you do it right away and without delay. You don't say, "I'll start obeying God in my sex life tomorrow." Delay is just one of many ways we seek to retain our autonomy and self-sovereignty. Here's how delay operates.

You're flirting with a woman at work and it has become a bit sexual. You know you shouldn't be doing it, but you sit down with her again in the lunch room and tell yourself that you'll cut it off tomorrow.

You're heart is pounding as you're surfing toward that porn site, hoping your wife doesn't wake up. You know you have no business being there, but to ease your guilt you tell yourself this is the last time.

You're seventeen and you're in the local park at night with your girlfriend. You've got your hand inside her bra. Your hand is shaking with a combination of excitement and fear. You know that what you're doing is wrong for you and for her, but you couldn't resist one more time. You tell yourself you'll break it off with her in the next few days.

You're living with a woman who is not your wife and you've recently committed yourself to Christ. You know you should not be sleeping with your girlfriend, but you tell yourself it will be such a hassle to separate and find separate apartments. You'll deal with it, but you can't handle it right now.

You know you've gotten yourself hooked on a series you have no business watching. It leaves you thinking in ways that are not pure, but you tell yourself that you'll finish out the season and not watch the new season in the fall.

Delay is disobedience in a tuxedo. Delay gives you room to rebel against the authority of God while telling yourself that you have every intention to obey, and in so doing you've eased your conscience when it actually needs to be troubled.

Your sex life will always be a window on how your heart is responding to the inescapable authority of God.

SEX AND DISOBEDIENCE

It's important to understand that, like obedience, disobedience is not just a set of behaviors; it's first a condition of the heart. So it's important to understand the psychology or posture of the heart behind obedience.

Part of the psychology of disobedience is to somehow, someway, convince yourself that you're smarter than God. Your rules are better or more practical than his rules. Your desires are more legitimate than those he desires for you. What you've planned for yourself is better than what he has willed for you. Maybe it's just telling yourself that the sexual boundary that you're stepping over isn't such a big deal just this once. Or it doesn't make sense that you can't sleep with someone you love even if you aren't married. Or you reason that culture has evolved, that we know things we didn't know when the Bible was written; it doesn't make any sense to be controlled by outdated, culturally bound rules. Disobedience always involves placing more reliability and value on your wisdom than on God's. You make a choice to do what makes sense or appears attractive, regardless of what God has said on the topic. Your position, when it comes to the wisdom of God, is not one of submission; it is one of critique. Whether you know it or not, you're standing above God, willing to reject what comes from him, what makes no sense to you.

Disobedience not only claims greater wisdom; it claims ownership. You find doing what you want to do comfortable because you view your life as belonging to you. If your life belongs to you, then you are entitled to do with it what you want. Disobedience always has an ownership posture. It claims rights that no human being has. As we laid out in a previous chapter, God owns you and everything about you. Any posture of ownership is a delusion that will only expose you to danger. You don't have a right to your own body, because your body doesn't belong to you. Disobedience also requires your willingness to reject the moral law of God and write your own moral code. It gives you the authority

121

to determine what is right and wrong, good or bad, true or false. But this is an authority that only God has. One of the sweetest graces in the Old Testament is when God, who knows everything from origin to destiny, tells his newly redeemed people how he's created them to live. He did not design them to be morally self-guiding; he lovingly gives them the moral guidance they desperately need. You are always submitting to God's law, or you're writing your own laws.

Finally, disobedience involves easing your conscience by arguing all the time for the logic of what you're doing. You are able to be comfortable with stepping over God's boundaries because you are a very committed and skilled self-swindler. We all do it. We tell ourselves that we're the good guys, that what we're doing isn't really that bad, and that our little sins aren't technically sins at all. Self-swindling works to quiet your internal restraint system that tells you to say no when you want to say yes. Self-swindling works to dull the pain of a conscience that is under the conviction of the Holy Spirit. Self-swindling is trying to sell to yourself that you can be disobedient and still retain your allegiance to God.

I remember being a bit stunned in a moment of counseling when an unfaithful and adulterous man said to me, "You would understand what I did [speaking of his sexual relationship with another woman] if you lived with my wife." It was the old "my wife made me do it" argument. He was saying in desperation that he'd been driven to this act by the horrible woman he was forced to live with. This is what self-swindling does. It rejects personal responsibility and all the moral choices of heart that always lie behind doing what is wrong in the eyes of God, and it works to make us feel good about what God clearly says is not good.

JESUS WANTS YOUR BODY

Sex is never just about physical pleasure. Sex is never just about horizontal relationships. Sex is always about obedience. Your sex life is shaped either by a willing submission to the authority of God or by you taking authority over your life and body as if it belongs to you. There is no escape.

This issue of obedience extends to the most intimate uses of your body. It is here that Romans 12:1 is very helpful: "I appeal to you brothers, by the mercies of God, to present your bodies as a living sacrifice, holy and acceptable to God, which is your spiritual worship." It could not be stated more clearly and eloquently. This passage connects your body to worship and obedience. Worship of God means you willingly give your body to him. You forever forsake ownership of your body and what you do with it. You view your body as belonging to God—his for the using. And you commit yourself to an obedient use of your body, that is, to doing with your body only what is holy and acceptable in his sight, no matter what your passions, thoughts, or desires tell you. Sexual purity is found in the intentional sacrifice of your body to God—no longer your desire and your way, but according to his will and for his glory.

And it's important to understand that this is not God robbing you of life simply because he is in charge and he has the power. Paul puts all this in the context of God extending mercy to us. This is grace. In calling us to make this intentional body sacrifice, God is rescuing us from us and protecting us from the dangers of a world gone mad. And all of this reminds us that we need God's law, but we must understand its limits. God's law is effective in exposing our moral neediness; it works to give us moral tracks to run on, but it cannot transform us. The law has no ability to make our hearts willing and pure. If it could, the redeemer, Christ Jesus, wouldn't have had to come to live and die and rise again in our place.

So sexual purity doesn't begin with a commitment to keep God's law; it begins with a confession that you don't want to and you can't. It requires the confession of the selfishness and rebellion of your heart. It owns that often impurity is more attractive to you than purity. You see, if sexual impurity was just a matter of a wrong set of behaviors, then the move toward purity would just be a matter of replacing old behaviors with new and better ones. If sexual impurity were just a matter of the lust of the heart, then that would be the thing you would need to address. But the reality is that sexual impurity is rooted in things that are vastly deeper than wrong thoughts and wrong actions. Sexual impurity grows in the soil of the scary condition of the sinful heart. I struggle with sexual impurity in the same way I struggle with materialism or gluttony, because I struggle with something deeper. What is this deeper thing? I struggle with self-worship and self-rule. In my heart there are still ways in which I want to be at the center of my world, where what I want, feel, or think I need is more important to me than God's will or the real needs of those around me. There are ways in which I am so busy loving and worshiping me that I have little time or energy left to love God or others.

I grapple every day with self-worship, and because I do, I want to be sovereign over my own life. I want to rule my life and set up my own rules. I want to have what seems best to me, and I don't want God or others to get in the way. I cannot escape how sex exposes both of these things in my heart. My sex life is always shaped by who I worship and by whose rules I submit to.

So when I face the deeper struggle of sexual purity, you can't help me with a just a greater understanding of my sexual self, a clearer awareness of where I am susceptible to temptation, or a better system of accountability. For all the helpfulness of these things, they easily become asking the law to do what only grace can accomplish. What my struggle with sexual purity reveals is the degree to which I still need a fundamental renewal or transformation of my heart. It is only when I am worshiping God above everything else, loving my neighbor as myself, and willingly submitting to God's authority that I will be pure. In the most basic sense, when it comes to the sexual purity battle, I have met the enemy, and it is me. I am the greatest sexual danger to me. I am my greatest source of temptation. I am the source of my struggle. It is the self-worship and self-sovereignty that still live in my heart that cause me to be attracted and susceptible to the sexual temptations that are everywhere around me in this world that has gone sexually insane.

So does this leave me hopeless? No! God, who knows how deep my struggle is, has gifted me with the lavish provisions of his powerful rescuing and transforming grace.

Where does purity start? It starts by confessing your profound need and that you are unable to change what needs to be changed. Sexual purity doesn't begin with setting up a regimen for behavioral change. It begins with mourning the condition of your heart, and when you do, you can rest assured that you will be greeted with powerful grace because your Savior has promised that he will never turn his back when you come to him with a broken and contrite heart.

Without this deeper heart confession, behavioral reformation and community accountability won't ultimately free you.

9

SO WHERE DO WE
GO FROM HERE?

It was hard for him to remember when sex hadn't been a struggle. It was hard to remember a day when he hadn't been hit with guilt, shame, regret, and fear. It was hard for him to remember what it was like to feel free and normal. It was hard for him.

The world of sex had been opened up to him long before he was emotionally or spiritually mature enough to handle it. In middle school he fell in with a group of boys who had sex as their common interest. They knew little more than that women's bodies were different and interesting and well worth investigating. Their conversations were dirty and uninformed, but they were compelling to him. He found himself thinking about women's "parts" and about how to get the girls at school to show him stuff. It wasn't long before he was stealing men's magazines from the local drug store and hanging around the women's dressing rooms at the local department store.

His thoughts about hanging out with girls had little to do with relationship. He was on a constant search for the girls who would "put out," although he would've denied it if you had accused him. In high school he became more and more obsessed with and addicted to sex. It was to him identity, power, and pleasure that he could find no where else. He had a stash of paper and video pornography hidden at home and was always on the prowl outside of his home, but his parents had no idea. To them, his interest in girls was just a teenage boy being a teenage boy.

The first three years of college were made up of mandatory classes and a whole lot of drinking and sex. If not with a female college classmate, he would spend the weekend at local strip clubs. He had no idea of the deep emotional and spiritual trouble he was in. He had no concept of the damage that he was doing to his soul. In the fourth year of college he was invited to a party by a girl he thought was pretty hot, so he gladly accepted the invitation. What he didn't know was that the party was sponsored by a campus ministry. To him, it was not much of a party, but he kept accepting the girl's invitations to the ministry's gatherings because he was interested in her and was intrigued by what he was hearing. Although he wouldn't have been able to describe it, he was increasingly concerned about himself and about how he was living. He was feeling guilt and regret like he had never experienced in his life. He began to ask questions of the people in charge, and before long he had given his heart to the Lord.

Although on one hand he was filled with joy, on the other hand he felt as if he carried a heavy burden around with him every day. He knew he was God's child, and he knew he was forgiven, but he also soon knew that he wasn't free of sexual temptation. There were times when he missed the old days and times when he desperately wanted what he knew he couldn't have. But he didn't think it was possible to tell the Christians around him what he was struggling with. What would they think of him? What would they do? He decided there was no way to share with others his addiction. He would give himself to knowing his faith and trying better. He would get involved in all of the activities he could, and he would hang with the right people. He would read his Bible every morning and read and watch the right things throughout the day. He was on God's side, and he would kick this thing.

But he didn't kick it; it recaptured him. It started with titillating sites on the Internet, then more and more secret viewing of pornography and sneaking out to the occasional strip club. He felt scared and defeated but would not reach out for help; there just seemed to be no way. In the midst of this, there were ways in which he did grow and his life did change. He grew in biblical literacy and theological understanding. He involved himself in the ministries of the campus church. In the middle of his heart being torn in two different directions, he met his future wife. She was beautiful, pure, and spiritually mature. She almost seemed too good to be true. For him, it was as close as you could get to love at first sight, but it also made him afraid. What if she knew who he really was? What if she knew where he had been and what he had done? What if she ever found him looking at pornography—then what?

He decided two things. First, there was no way he was going to jeopardize the first good relationship of his life by telling her things she simply couldn't handle. He would never open up. He would avoid the need to answer direct questions. He would hide his struggle. Second, he told himself that he would turn the corner, that illicit sex was gone, in his past, never to return. And he knew how he would pull it off—marriage. Clearly, God had brought her into his life to help him defeat something he hadn't been able to defeat. The legitimate sexual relationship of marriage would liberate him from his desire to have illegitimate sex outside of marriage. He was so happy. He proposed, she accepted, and they married two months after graduation.

The first several months of marriage made him feel that he was free of the struggles of his past. The newness, freedom, and excitement of sex with his wife in the context of marriage kept his thoughts and desires focused. He began to think that he had turned the corner, that is, until that day at the mall. Not only did he notice that attractive woman and think things he hadn't thought in a while, but also he followed her around, hoping to see more. He left the mall devastated but still not willing to tell his secret. The next several years were a great struggle mixed with occasional times of freedom. But the draw was getting stronger, and he was living more and more of a double life. His wife had little idea and little concern. The only thing that bothered her was that they didn't have sex as often as they once had. He knew he was in trouble, but for all his belief in God's power, he didn't have much hope.

• • •

She had been the cheerleader, prom queen, and all around golden girl, but by her own admission and in her own words she had been a slut. She loved to be the tease. She loved the power of seduction. She loved hearing guys beg. She loved dressing a bit provocatively, and she loved being noticed. She loved having the body that men wanted to touch. She loved being the center of attention, and if sex was the way to get to the center, then so be it.

High school was all about being the girl everyone wanted or wanted to be. It was all about sexually teasing her male classmates and making out in the car with a selected few. She liked her body and the fact that men liked it too, and she grew more and more comfortable with using her body to get what she wanted. It all seemed to be the life of her dreams until the end of college. She wanted to get married but had little idea that marriage would be the end of the lifestyle that got her up in the morning and kept her going.

Once she had the man, the pattern of tease, conquest, and seduction was over. Sex for her had not been an expression of commitment and love. It had been about personal power and pleasure. So she found sex in marriage neither exciting nor attractive. Sure, it was exciting at first, but it soon became mundane and boring.

She found herself flirting at work or in the grocery store. It was wrong, but it was exciting. She employed the double meaning, stood closer to men than she should, and dressed to get attention. More and more she felt trapped by her marriage. More and more she was distant from her husband. And that day when she kissed her fellow worker in the stockroom, she knew she was in trouble. The problem was that she didn't know what to do. She wanted what she could not have and didn't want what she had been given. And on top of it all, she was convinced that if she was honest about her past and her present struggle, she would lose everything. She decided to keep silent and to quit messing around, but her feelings and the temptations didn't go away.

THE GOSPEL OF JESUS CHRIST AND SEX

Perhaps these stories touch your story or perhaps not. The fact is that many Christians are in the midst of some kind of personal sexual struggle or dysfunction. There are many married couples in the church who do not experience the beautiful, intimate sexual oneness that God designed. There are many professing Christian men who are living a double life. There are many Christian singles who are succumbing to temptations they are called to fight. There are many Christians whose minds wander daily and whose desires regularly go astray. And many of these brothers and sisters in the faith live in fearful secrecy and silence. They know theologically that Jesus died for their sins and that embedded in his death are the promises of forgiveness and freedom, but they simply do not know how to get from where they are to where they need to be.

They know that the hope of defeating sin is the reason that Jesus came, but this isn't just sin—you know, like lying or cheating. It's different. It's private. It's shame-inducing. It's just not something you talk about. In reality they stare at the empty cross of Jesus, and for them it seems that's exactly what it is—empty. It's empty of hope and help for them, so they live in silence. They minimize the depth of their struggle, and they determine that tomorrow they'll do better. Or they've already given up and given in, and they hope that in the end Jesus will forgive them.

In a world that has gone sexually insane, we have to do better. We have to quit being silent. We have to help one another connect the transforming power of the gospel of Jesus Christ to sex and to sexual sin and struggle. The silence must be broken. Biblical hope must be given. People need to be called out of hiding. People need to believe and act as if change really is possible. More of us need to be experiencing the forgiveness, freedom, hope, and courage of the gospel.

This is what this chapter is about. It's meant to look at sex and sexual struggle through the hope-stimulating lens of the grace of the Lord Jesus Christ. Let's jump in. The person and work of the Lord Jesus Christ means the following.

1) You don't have to be ashamed that you're a sexual being.

We have to start here. What the cross teaches us is that sex is not a problem; it is a gift. Jesus didn't suffer and die to free you from sex but to free you from sexual sin. You must never give way to cursing your sexuality, because the same one who wisely created your sexuality came to be your Savior. He didn't come to fill you with guilt because you are sexual but to free you from your bondage to and guilt from sexual sin. Your sexuality points to his glory as creator and to the amazing creature that you are. It is something that the cross allows you to celebrate, because it is the grace of the cross that gives you the power to keep sex in its proper place in your heart and in your life.

Your problem and mine is not primarily that we are sexual beings, or is it primarily that we tend to love the creation more than the Creator so that we use God's good gifts in ways they were not created to be used. That's because sexual sin and struggle is not first a matter of what we do with our body. It's first a matter of what we do with our heart. The great Puritan teacher and preacher Richard Sibbes wrote powerfully of this struggle:

> Again, if you will preserve tenderness of heart, take need of
> spiritual drunkenness; that is, that you be not drunk with the

immoderate use of created things; of setting your love too much upon outward things. For what says the prophet, "Wine and women take away the heart" (Hosea 4:11); that is, the immoderate use of any earthly things takes away the spiritual sense; for the more sensible the soul is of outward things, the less it is of spiritual. For as the outward takes away the inward heat, so the love of one thing abates the love of another. The setting of too much love on earthly things takes away the sense of better things, and hardens the heart. When the heart is filled with the pleasures and profits of this life, it is not sensible of any judgment that hangs over the head; as in the old world, they ate and drank, they married and gave in marriage, they bought and sold, while the flood came upon them and swept all away (Matthew 24:17). When a man sets his love upon created things, the very strength of his soul is lost. . . . Talk of religion to a carnal man, whose senses are lost with the love of earthly things, he has no ear for that; his sense is quite lost, he has no relish or [savor] for anything good. Talk to a covetous man, that has his soul set upon the things of this life, he has no relish of anything else; his heart is already so hardened to get honour or wealth. Though it be to the ruin of others, that he cares not how hard it has become. Therefore we are bidden to take heed that our hearts be not overcome with drunkenness and the cares of this life, for those will make a man insensible of spiritual things (Luke 21:43).

Applying to sex what Sibbes says about the heart highlights what is important. The struggle of sexual purity is not so much a struggle with sex but with the proneness of our hearts to wander, that is, with the tendency of every sinner to look for fulfillment of heart where it cannot be found. As long as you are looking for life in the creation, you won't be seeking it in the Creator. Sex is a good and beautiful thing, but desire for this good thing becomes a bad and dangerous thing when it becomes a heart-controlling thing. The idolatry of the sinful heart is the problem. So when you ask sex to satisfy you, you have to go back again and again because the satisfaction of sex is powerful but frighteningly short-lived. Asking the creation to be your savior always ends in addiction of some kind.

You don't have to be ashamed of your sexuality, but you must guard your heart as you live out your sexuality.

2) You don't have to deny that you're a sinner.

So much of what propels personal and cultural sexual insanity is active, regular, long-term self-denial. Self-righteousness is simply insane itself, but it's there in all of us. The grace of the cross of Jesus Christ means we don't have to deny reality anymore. We don't have to work to make ourselves and others think that we are righteous. We don't have to recast what we have done to make it look better. We don't have to work to make acceptable to our consciences what God says is wrong. We don't have to argue that we are okay when we are not okay. Grace means we do not have to be afraid of what will be uncovered or exposed about us, because whatever is revealed has already been fully covered by the blood of Jesus.

This means that you don't have to deny your struggle for sexual purity. You don't have to act as if you're pure if you're not pure. You don't have to lie to yourself or others. You don't have to work to make lust look like something less than lust. You don't have to tell yourself that your sex life is okay when it is not okay in the eyes of God. Honesty is possible because grace is available. Facing the depth of your sexual struggle is possible because you do not face that struggle alone; your Savior is ever with you. You and I must remember that self-denial is never a doorway to personal change. The grace of Jesus Christ welcomes you to live in the courage of honesty, knowing that there is grace for every dark and dangerous thing that will be exposed. The way you deal with your struggle for sexual purity changes when you embrace the fact that grace means you don't have to deny your struggle anymore.

But there is one more point to be made here. The Bible never presents sexual sin as being of a different nature than other sins. Sexual sin may have different social and interpersonal consequences, but it is sin, no more no less. In Romans 1 sexual sin is listed along with envy, gossip, and deceit, even with something as mundane as disobedience to parents. That is why this is important. If you begin to think that sexual sin is sin of a different kind or nature, it is logical then to wonder if the same biblical promises, hopes, and provisions apply to it.

I sat with a woman who had struggled for years with homosexuality while she said to me in tears, "No one treated me as if I was just a sinner. I thought my sin was different and what worked for others wouldn't work for me. It is wonderful to say that all sexual sin is sin, sin for which Christ died." Sexual sin sits inside the circle of the rescuing, forgiving, transforming, and delivering grace of the Lord Jesus Christ. It is a deceitful, lying enemy who would work to convince you that the provisions of the cross can't help you because sexual sin is different. In our struggle for sexual purity, each of us must reject that lie.

3) You don't have to deny the fallenness of the world around you.

You don't have to act as if life is easy and your struggles are few. You don't have to act as though you live a life free from temptation. You can admit that troubling temptation leaves you weary and sometimes confused. You can cry out for help when you are tired, distressed, or have lost the fight once again. It is right at moments to be angry at what the world around you has become. It is right to be sad that things around you are as broken as they are. You should hate the fact that sex seems to infect almost everything you encounter. You must face the fact that this right-here, right-now world will never be the paradise that your heart longs for. Paradise is coming, but this is not it.

You should be sad that the purity of your heart is always under assault by the seductive voices of evil that are all around. You should be angry that the sanctity and purity of your marriage must be protected because your marriage is located in a world where temptation is everywhere. It should not be okay for you. You should not grow comfortable with the sorry state of things. You should be angry that God's beautiful gift of sexuality has been so deluded and distorted. You should hate the fact that we have gone sexually crazy. And you should groan and mourn before your Savior, who hears and cares.

The words of Romans 8 are helpful to read as Paul connects the gospel of Jesus Christ to being honest about the brokenness of the surrounding world:

> I consider that our present sufferings are not worth comparing with the glory that will be revealed in us. For the creation waits in eager expectation for the children of God to be revealed. For the creation was subjected to frustration, not by its own choice, but by the will of the one who subjected it, in hope that the creation itself will be liberated from its bondage to decay and brought into the freedom and glory of the children of God. We know that the whole creation has been groaning as in the pains of childbirth right up to the present time. Not only so, but we ourselves, who have the firstfruits of the Spirit, groan inwardly as we wait eagerly for our adoption to sonship, the redemption of our bodies. For in this hope we were saved. But hope that is seen is no hope at all. Who hopes for what they already have? But if we hope for what we do not yet have, we wait for it patiently. In the same way, the Spirit helps us in our weakness. We do not know what we ought to pray for, but the Spirit himself intercedes for us through wordless groans. And he who searches our hearts knows the mind of the Spirit, because the Spirit intercedes for God's people in accordance with the will of God. And we know that in all things God works for the good of those who love him, who have been called according to his purpose. For those God foreknew he also predestined to be conformed to the image of his Son, that he might be the firstborn among many brothers and sisters. And those he predestined, he also called; those he called, he also justified; those he justified, he also glorified. What, then, shall we say in response to these things? If God is for us, who can be against us? He who did not spare his own Son, but gave him up for us all—how will he not also, along with him, graciously give us all things? Who will bring any charge against those whom God has chosen? It

is God who justifies. Who then is the one who condemns? No one. Christ Jesus who died—more than that, who was raised to life—is at the right hand of God and is also interceding for us. Who shall separate us from the love of Christ? Shall trouble or hardship or persecution or famine or nakedness or danger or sword? As it is written:

> "For your sake we face death all day long;
>   we are considered as sheep to be slaughtered."

No, in all these things we are more than conquerors through him who loved us. For I am convinced that neither death nor life, neither angels nor demons, neither the present nor the future, nor any powers, neither height nor depth, nor anything else in all creation, will be able to separate us from the love of God that is in Christ Jesus our Lord. (vv. 18–39 NIV)

Paul argues here that because you have been blessed with the unshakable love of the Lord Jesus Christ, you can face the struggles of life in this fallen world with honesty and hope. Biblical faith never requires you to deny reality. Honesty about struggles within and temptations without is necessary if you are going to live in sexual purity.

4) You don't have to hide in guilt and fear.

One of the saddest moments in Scripture is found in Genesis 3. For the very first time, you find Adam and Eve hiding in fear from their Creator. Designed for life-long and life-shaping communion with him, they are now afraid to face him. You know right away that something horrible has happened. Hiding from someone that you say you love is never a good sign. Hiding because of guilt and fear is a red flag that something has gone very wrong. Hiding a problem seldom leads to the solution for the problem. Lying to others about your problem never leads to their understanding and assistance. You hide when you tell yourself you're okay. You hide when you minimize your struggle. You hide when you lie to others. You hide when you give nebulous nonanswers to people who are trying to help you. You hide when you try to cover your struggle by making yourself look more spiritual than you are. You hide when you convince yourself that you can do alone what you will only ever do with the help of God and others.

The cross of Jesus Christ welcomes you out of hiding, because on the cross Jesus endured your punishment, he carried your guilt, he bore your shame, and he endured your rejection. He did all of this so that you wouldn't have to hide from God. He did all of this so that in your sin, weakness, and failure you could run toward a holy God and not away from him. He did all of this so that you could live in the light and not lurk around in the darkness. He did all of this so that you would find mercy and grace in your time of need. So step out of hiding and reach out for help. Your Savior endured the rejection you and I should have received so that even in our failure, we will never see God turn and walk away from us. Now, that's grace!

5) You don't have to fight your battle alone.

The dark secrecy of sexual sin can make you feel alienated, misunderstood, rejected, and alone. You can fall into thinking that no one will ever understand, that no one will ever want to be near you or help you. The privacy of the double life of many who are struggling with sexual sin can make them feel separated from the closest people in their life. If you are God's child, it is impossible for you to be alone. Let me make this distinction: it's not impossible for you to *feel* alone, but it is impossible for you to *be* alone. You and I must distinguish between the power of what we feel and the realities that should shape the way we act and respond.

Here's where the message of Scripture is so incredibly encouraging. God's greatest gift to us is the gift of himself. What changes the whole ballgame is his presence. The wisdom principles of Scripture wouldn't be worth the paper they are printed on if it weren't for the powerful rescuing and transforming presence of the Redeemer. Without him with us, for us, and in us, we wouldn't understand the principles, we wouldn't desire to live inside them, and we wouldn't have the power to do so if we wanted to. Our hope for change is a person, the Lord Almighty.

You will notice as you read the Bible that every time God's people faced seemingly insurmountable difficulty, God didn't work to pump up their self-confidence. Rather, he reminded them of his presence. When God called Moses to confront Pharaoh, the most powerful ruler on earth, and Moses was afraid to go, God said, "I will be with you" (Ex. 3:12). When God called Joshua to lead Israel to defeat the warring nations of Palestine, God reminded Joshua that he was with him wherever he went. (Josh 1:5, 9). When Gideon was scared to death at the thought of leading Israel against the pirate nation of Midian, God said, "The Lord is with you." (Judg. 6:12). When God called David to be king over a defeated and divided Israel, God reminded David that he had been with him and encouraged him that he would continue. (2 Sam. 7:9). When Jesus sent out his novice disciples to take the gospel to a world that didn't want it, he reminded them that he would be with them always. (Matt. 28:20). And as you and I struggle with sexual purity in a world that has gone sexually insane, God says to us, "I will never leave you nor forsake you" (Heb. 13:5). As God's child it is impossible to fight the battle for purity by yourself, because you have been indwelt by a warrior Spirit who fights on your behalf, even when you don't have the sense to call on him.

But there is more. God has placed us in his church because he knows that our journey to sexual purity is a community project. We were not designed to know ourselves clearly, to identify the places where change is needed, and to fight for that change by ourselves. As Paul says in Ephesians 4:16, it is "every joint" that does its part as the body of Christ grows to maturity. If you want to be sexually pure, you need people to help you see yourself in ways that sin blinds you to. If you want to gain ground, you need people who will confront you when you are rebelling and encourage you when you are weak. And most of all, you need people who will remind you again and again of the powerful presence of your Redeemer and the lavish provisions of his grace.

You and I will never defeat sexual sin and live in restful purity if we attempt to do what we're not hardwired to do—fight the battle all by ourselves.

6) You don't have to question God's patient love.

Could there be any greater encouragement for us as we are confronted with the fickleness of our hearts, our weakness in the face of temptations, the rebellion that causes us to do what is wrong even when we know it is wrong, and the places where we arrogantly think that we know better than God, than the gospel declaration that nothing can separate us from the love of God in Christ Jesus? God's love is yours forever, not because you will be faithful but because he is. God's love is constant, not because you earned it in your righteousness but because God knew it was the only hope for you in your unrighteousness. God's love never wanes even when your allegiance to him does, because it is not based on your performance but on his character.

Here's the point: if you think that God's love is at stake, that he will withdraw it when you mess up, then in your moment of failure you will run from him and not to him. But if you really believe in your deepest moment of sexual foolishness, weakness, failure, or rebellion that when you run to him, he will greet you with arms of redemptive love, then it makes no sense to hide from him or to separate yourself from his care. Here is the bottom line: in your struggle with sex, your love for God is never your hope. Hope is to be found only ever in his love for you. Since he loves you, he wants what's best for you and will work to defeat the enemies of your soul until the last enemy has been defeated and your struggle is no more.

7) You can quit thinking that change is impossible.

Because of all that has been said above, you are free to quit thinking of sexual sin as impossible to defeat. I cannot tell you how many people I have counseled who were dealing with some form of sexual struggle and were functionally hopeless. They hadn't yet abandoned their formal theology, but they had lost all hope that the truths of that theology would have any impact on their lives. They had begun to succumb to the depressing perspective that what they were dealing with was impossible to defeat. In fact, some of them said something like this to me: "I've seen other people defeat sins in their lives, and I've seen some things change in my own, but not this one. No matter how hard I try and no matter how faithfully I pray, nothing seems to change."

But here is the truth: because what you are dealing with is sin, because that is exactly what Christ died to defeat, because you are never alone while Christ fights on your behalf, because he has blessed you with mercies that are new every morning, and because he has surrounded you with protective and restorative resources of the body of Christ, you are not encased in concrete. You can change. You can be pure. Change is not a theological fantasy. It is the bright promise of the cross of Jesus Christ. There will be a day when you will struggle no more. Why not reject hopelessness and move in that direction right now?

8) You can live in a new and better way.

So, if by grace change really is possible, then the only logical response is to get up in the morning in the courage of faith and begin to address things in your sexual life where change is indicated. Perhaps the following questions will help you.

- Where and how do you regularly set yourself up for failure?
- Where do you tend to make foolish choices?
- Where do you expose yourself to things that are not helpful?
- Where do you tend to tell yourself that you're okay when you're not?

- What are the things you say to yourself that allow you to remain hopeless?
- Where do you look wrong in the face and do it anyway?
- Where and when are you most susceptible to give in to temptation?
- Where are you asking physical, sexual pleasure to satisfy your heart?
- In what ways do you tend to minimize your struggle?
- With whom are you being less than honest?
- Are there moments when you still allow yourself to question God's love?

Now, you know that none of these questions will rescue you from temptation and make you pure. They simply don't have the power to do that. But they can be used to help you understand your struggle, to begin to think about what a new and better way looks like, and to identify places where you need to reach out for help. In other words, the questions can function as tools in the hands of a God of glorious grace, who alone has the power to defeat sin in your life and mature you into a person who is pure of heart and hands.

You see, it is only the gospel of Jesus that has the power to bring sanity to sexuality in a world gone crazy and within this power the potential for real, lasting, personal transformation. Yes, you can live a God-honoring sexual life in a world gone crazy. Yes, you really can.

10

MONEY MATTERS

Money matters—there is just no getting around it. It is not un-spiritual to think about it, to be concerned about it, or to talk of it often. In a very significant way your life will be shaped by what you think about money, and in a way that is inescapable, some-how, someway, your heart will struggle with money. Money is a big deal, but even a bigger deal in a world that seems to have gone financially insane. Money is such a big deal that in Christ's teach-ing ministry, it was one of his favorite and most important topics. Rather than avoiding money matters or talking about them with timidity, like many pastors do, Jesus talked about the topic all the time. You may not know it, but Jesus talked about money more than he talked about heaven. He talked about money more than he talked about hell. Of the thirty-nine parables recorded in the Gospels, eleven of them talk about money. Almost every page of the Gospel of Luke is dyed with this conversation.

This conversation about money is not just there in the minis-try of Jesus but is a significant theme throughout all of Scripture. The biblical discussion of money tends to divide itself into two categories: the danger of money and the blessing of money. Hear the power of the warning in these passages about the dangers of money.

> For the love of money is a root of all kinds of evils. It is through this craving that some have wandered away from the faith and pierced themselves with many pangs. (1 Tim. 6:10–11)

For where your treasure is, there will your heart be also. (Luke 12:34)

Put no trust in extortion;
  set no vain hope on robbery;
  if riches increase, set not your heart on them. (Ps. 62:10)

He who loves money will not be satisfied with money, nor he who loves wealth with his income; this also is vanity. (Eccles. 5:10)

But those who desire to be rich fall into temptation, into a snare, into many senseless and harmful desires that plunge people into ruin and destruction. (1 Tim. 6:9)

Better is a little with righteousness
  than great revenues with injustice. (Prov. 16:8)

Keep your life free from love of money, and be content with what you have, for he has said, "I will never leave you nor forsake you." (Heb. 13:5)

Do not toil to acquire wealth;
  be discerning enough to desist. (Prov. 23:4)

A faithful man will abound with blessings,
  but whoever hastens to be rich will not go unpunished.
    (Prov. 28:20)

The Bible also points us to the blessing that money can be. Here Scripture tends to emphasize the good that can be done with money and the way that money is a revealer of the heart:

A rich man's wealth is his strong city;
  the poverty of the poor is their ruin. (Prov. 10:15)

You shall give to him freely [the poor brother], and your heart shall not be grudging when you give to him, because for this the LORD your God will bless you in all your work and in all that you undertake. (Deut. 15:10)

Bring the full tithe into the storehouse, that there may be food in my house. And thereby put me to the test, says the LORD of hosts, if I will not open the windows of heaven for you and pour down for you a blessing until there is no more need. (Mal. 3:10)

Honor the LORD with your wealth
 and with the firstfruits of all your produce;
then your barns will be filled with plenty,
 and your vats will be bursting with wine. (Prov. 3:9–10)

It is more blessed to give than to receive. (Acts 20:25b)

The rich rules over the poor,
 and the borrower is the slave of the lender. (Prov. 22:7)

One who is faithful in a very little is also faithful in much, and one who is dishonest in a very little is also dishonest in much. If then you have not been faithful in the unrighteous wealth, who will entrust to you the true riches? (Luke 16:10–11)

What causes quarrels and what causes fights among you? Is it not this, that your passions are at war within you? You desire and do not have, so you murder. You covet and cannot obtain, so you fight and quarrel. . . . You ask and do not receive, because you ask wrongly, to spend it on your passions. (James 4:1–3)

Money is a powerful thing. On one hand, it can expose me to danger, while on the other hand it can be used of God to reveal the need of my heart and, through me, to bless the lives of others. You and I will interact with money in some way. That interaction is one of the things that will set the direction of our lives. When it comes to money, Scripture leaves little room for comfortable neutrality.

Money will be a blessing to you, or it will be a curse. It will be a tool in the hands of a God of grace, or it will be a doorway to bad and dangerous things. Like two sides of a physical coin, there are two spiritual sides to money. Each side calls to you. Each side holds before you a vision and promises. Each side asks not just for the investment of your money but for the allegiance of your heart. The battle between the two sides of the money coin wages in the heart of every person this side of eternity. Money *is* a danger. Money *is* a blessing. What will it be for you? Where the rubber meets the road in everyday life, you will not answer the question once. No, you will have to answer it again and again as day after day you are greeted with false promises and truth, each voice telling you what to do with the money in your hand.

Your Lord talked about these issues as often as he did because he knows well the power and importance of money issues. He knows how significant this heart battle is for you and me. He knows how easily seduced we can be. When it comes to money, he knows how quickly we can lose our way. He knows how susceptible we are to give the love of our hearts to money. And if we listen to our Lord, we will know that this is a conversation we need to have.

You will walk with your money, no matter how much you have, down a pathway of danger or blessing. Very important things in your life will be shaped by the pathway you take. As with sex, to walk the pathway of blessing takes more than good theology and knowledge of biblical commands and principles. It takes powerful rescuing grace. As we examine money as a danger and as a blessing, every word I have written is from the knowledge that, when it comes to money, our hearts will only rest contented when they have been rescued by and are being protected by God's amazing grace.

There is one more thing that needs to be said about the blessing-danger battle of money. The war of money is not first a battle about the amount of money you make or the degree to which you have constructed a rational budget to follow. No, this battle is a deeply spiritual battle. The fact is that human beings need more than information and administration in order that lives be what God designed them to be, because their problems are deeper than ignorance and disorganization. As I have written before, human beings live out of their hearts. It is the thoughts and desires of our heart that set the direction of our life. So, whatever amount of money we have, our relationship to and use of money will be determined by how our heart interacts with money.

Let me explain. There are four things that work together to soften the heart for money problems. These four things set up the heart to do what must never be done with money: love it. (The love of money, what that means and what it does, will be the content of the next chapter). What are the things that weaken the resolve of the heart and set it up for money difficulties? The first is *ingratitude*. A grateful heart is a heart at rest. A grateful person is aware that he deserves nothing that he possesses and enjoys. Because of this, he daily counts his blessings and is thankful for the little things that would otherwise be taken for granted. The unthankful person is doing just the opposite. He keeps telling himself that he deserves more than he has. Because of this, he is way more aware of what he doesn't yet have than all of the things he has been graciously given. This causes him to live an entitled and demanding life. Never quite satisfied, he easily justifies a wasteful and selfish use of money.

The second ingredient is *need*. This is one of the most poorly and overused words in human culture. The majority of what we are able to tell ourselves we need, we don't actually need. We all are very skilled at loading our desires into our need category, and once we have, we think it's our right to have these things, and therefore it's appropriate to do what is necessary to posses them. So we waste all kinds of money satisfying needs that aren't really needs, all the while feeling quite comfortable because if it's a need, it seems right to acquire it. So with closets bursting with more clothes than we can wear and refrigerators filled with more than we can eat and houses bigger than we actually need, we are still able to tell ourselves that we are needy. And because we have told ourselves that we are needy, we will spend more.

Along with ingratitude and need there is a third thing that weakens the defenses of the heart against the love of money: *discontent*. Because I am not grateful for all the things I have been given and don't deserve, and because I have misdiagnosed need, loading many things in my need category that are not needs, I am a constantly discontented person. It will be virtually impossible to be satisfied with what I have, so I will be on a constant quest for more. Since I am on a constant quest for more, I will tend to spend more than I should to satisfy my discontent, but because my discontent is rooted in ingratitude and misunderstood need, spending more won't solve my problem. So, I will end up spending more than I have, because what I am trying to do can't work. Contentment isn't a money problem, a physical possession, or a location problem; it's a problem of the heart and therefore is not solved by spending.

The final ingredient that works with ingratitude, need, and discontent to set up your heart to put money in a place it must never be is *envy*. If you are unthankful and convinced that you deserve more, if you have been able to convince yourself that there are things you need that you do not have, and this has left you deeply discontent, you will invariably look over the fence and envy the person who appears to have what you have not yet been able to acquire and enjoy. Envious people are always taking account. Envious people are always comparing. Envious people are constantly placing things on their "he has, but I don't" list. Envious people regularly feel that they have been given a bad deal, and it is right for them to use their resources to settle the score. Envy will cause you to be both self-oriented and foolish in your use of money.

It is ingratitude, neediness, discontent, and envy of the heart that cause me to be all too money conscious, all too self-focused in my use of it, and all too liberal in my expenditure of it. My life really will end up being "money, money, money" no matter how much of it I actually have. You see, the problem with money is not that it exists. The problem with money is not that you have too little or too much. Money problems are always heart problems; they're deeper than the size of your paycheck and the specificity of your budget. Money can be a blessing or a curse. Let's consider what both sides look like.

MONEY IS A BLESSING

1) Money is a window on the goodness of God.

James says it very well, "Every good gift and every perfect gift is from above, coming down from the Father of lights with whom there is no variation or shadow due to change" (James 1:17). If you allow yourself in a me-istic and materialistic culture to think with a moment of sanity, you will know that what James says is verified and demonstrated by your experience. If you have sufficient money to meet your daily needs, there is no way that you have controlled all the circumstances, locations, and relationships necessary to to have that money. You may protest, "But Paul, I went out and got my job, and I have worked hard every day." Yes, but you didn't create the natural gifts that are necessary to qualify for and to do your work; you surely didn't create the economic conditions necessary for the job to be available, and you definitely were not in control of the decision-making capacity of the person who hired you.

If we think with a humble and sound mind, it only makes sense that every good thing in our life is the result of the loving-kindness of one who is control of the details and who has blessed us with things we could not have achieved, earned, or deserved. Money can sit in our heart as another evidence of the grace of God, grace so tender and faithful that we continue to experience blessings even on our worst day. Money is meant to function as an arrow pointing to the goodness and faithfulness of God.

And even when money is lean, we are reminded of how dependent we are on someone bigger than us, and how thankful we should be that we are not alone in these lean circumstances.

149

2) Money is a window on what rules your heart.

When you get unexpected money, what is the first thing you want to do with it? Luella and I were in our early days of ministry with two hungry children, barely making it on the meager salary our little church was able to pay us. I must admit that in those days I struggled a lot with envy and often wondered what in the world God was doing. One afternoon an unexpected and anonymous envelope came in the mail with a $100 check in it. Before that check was completely out of the envelope I had spent it seven ways. I ran and showed it to Luella. It seemed to me like a million dollars. She looked at it for a moment, and then she looked up at me and said, "You know, Paul, we're doing okay and we weren't expecting this money. Why don't we give it to someone less fortunate?" I couldn't believe what I was hearing! I thought that this was the big one—my wife had gone nuts! I watched as that checked slipped through my fingers and begrudgingly gave it to a poor family in our church.

When you have extra money, what do you dream of buying? In the use of your money, does it make you happier to use it for your own purposes and pleasure or to offer it to God for his purposes and the work of his kingdom? Do you find it is way easier to get than it is to give? Do you envy the person next to you who has resources you don't have? Do you tend to spend more than you should while telling yourself that you would give more if you could? Does the level of your contentment rise and fall with the amount of money that's in your wallet? Are you able to celebrate what you've been given while at the same time looking without compassion at someone clearly needier than you? Are you ready, willing, and quick to give? Do you look for need that you can alleviate with resources that you don't really need? Are you glad to give, even in seasons when you don't have much?

Money is a very accurate window on what is truly important to us. It exposes the fact that this side of eternity it is really hard to hold in our hearts as important what God says is truly important. There is a dangerous tendency in each of our hearts for things to increase in importance, beyond their true importance, and begin to command the thoughts, desires, and allegiance of our hearts. If you're humbly willing to look, your desires for and use of money will help you see what is battling for the rulership of your heart.

3) Money is a window on the dangers of the fallen world.

Money is a doorway to danger. There are few greater dangers in this fallen world than to listen to the myriad voices that tell us that somehow, someway, satisfaction of heart can be found in the possession of or experience of something in creation. Money can be one of those things, or it can be what enables us to experience one of those things. It goes like this: "If only I had this much money, then I would be satisfied." Or, "If only I could afford, then I would be content."

Money, what it can do and what it can supply, reminds me that this is a world of deceit and danger. Things are not always what they seem. And in this world of deceit and danger there is no more dangerous lie than the one says that life can be found somewhere outside of the Creator. How many people have believed that lie and have ended with both heart and wallet empty? The struggle with money in each of our hearts is a constant reminder that we still live in a danger zone. The war still goes on, and we must be willing to fight until the last enemy is under the foot of the Lord of grace, who will usher us into a place where the danger is no more.

4) Money is a means of responding to the needs of others.

It may seem obvious, but it is worth noting that money provides a wonderful means of blessing others. There is a way in which you and I are always viewing ourselves as either a container or a conduit for the money that we are given. Either we want it to stop with us because we have conceived many ways that money will make our life better, easier, or more pleasurable, or we think of ourselves as a pipeline and are excited that the money we have been given can bless and benefit the lives of others. Either our money is the currency that pays the bills for the small-market visions of the kingdom of self, or it is a God-given tool in our hands for participating in the big-picture work of the kingdom of God. If we were honest, most of us would have to say that, when it comes to money, we live quite inconsistently. Sometimes we are excited by the greater purposes of God's kingdom, and in those moments we are cheerful givers. Other times we are quite full of ourselves and can't think of anything better to do with our money than to spend it on ourselves. God hasn't provided for us simply to provide for us, but in providing for us, he has enabled us to be a means of his provision for others.

5) Money can connect you to the work of the bigger kingdom.

I've already said it, but I want to emphasize it by making it a separate point: your world of money will be determined by your allegiance to the work of one of two kingdoms: the kingdom of God or the kingdom of self. God gives you money not so much to make sure that your kingdom works, but to connect you by grace to the work of a much bigger, much better kingdom. As you give yourself to the work of this kingdom, you get to watch your money do things that are literally of eternal consequence. In offering your resources to the bigger kingdom, your money is used to fuel the most important work in the universe—redemption.

MONEY CAN BE A DANGEROUS THING

1) Money can cause you to forget God.

Physical neediness can cause you to cry out to God for help, and as you cry out for help you come to realize that you need it not only physically but also spiritually. A pastor of a church in an extremely affluent community told me that since his people are able to buy their way into or out of just about anything, it is hard for them to think of themselves as needy. The supposed self-reliance of wealth can tempt us to believe in the larger delusion of our autonomy—that we have a right to live life as we want—and our self-sufficiency—that we have within ourselves all we need to be what we're supposed to be and to do what we're supposed to do. Money can allow us to afford a self-centered way of living that acts as if nothing is greater than us and more important than our individual wants, needs, and feelings.

Now, don't get me wrong here. There is no teaching in Scripture that would lead us to believe that poor people are better off spiritually than others. My point is to alert you to one of the dangers of money. Money can function as an ingredient in a lifestyle that, at street level, forgets God's existence and his plan. This lifestyle is more about personal glory than God's glory, and it reduces one's expenditure of money to personal desire, self-defined need, and the pursuit of individual comfort and pleasure. You may not have theologically denied the existence of God, but your money supports a lifestyle that ignores it.

2) Money can change the way you think about you.

Money is a stimulant. It will be used to stimulate a Godward way of life or an inward way of life. A friend told me that for years he had prided himself on being committed to and content with a "simple" lifestyle, that is, until he came into money. Suddenly he found himself wanting the more luxurious car; he was attracted to the more expensive shirt, and he wanted to eat at the better restaurant. He said, "It was humbling to admit that I wasn't living the simple life because I was spiritually committed to it. I was living the simple life because I was poor." Money can encourage you to be more self-focused and demanding; it can edge you toward being discontent with what once made you content, and, even more dangerous, money can move you to begin to expect from life what you should not expect and feel that you deserve what you do not deserve. Money really can have a huge influence on how you define yourself and how you think about your life and on the expectations that shape your disappointments.

3) Money can cause you to look down on others.

What was going on was very clear and very sad. The affluent kids stood around and made fun of a homeless man who was doing his best to get out of their way. What was the difference between the kids and the homeless man? Well, in the deepest and most profound way, there was nothing different. The kids and the homeless guy were both made in the image of God and made to reflect his glory. They were all sinners in desperate need of redemption. Neither the homeless man nor the affluent teenagers had been in charge of all the circumstances that led them to where they were in their lives. Neither the kids nor the man could stand before God and say they deserve anything. But the boys didn't see themselves as similar to the man. They saw themselves as a higher order of human being, and they treated the poor man as less than human.

What caused them to think the way they thought and to treat the man the way they did? Well, there are many answers to that question, too many for us to consider here, but there was one major ingredient that fueled it all—money. To those suburban high school boys, this man was a vagrant, a bum, a loser. They were the chosen ones. It was ugly and mean, but it pictured one of the dangers of money. As it redefines your identity, it can also change the way you look at others. Money can stimulate the prideful prejudice that lurks somewhere in the heart of every sinner.

4) Money can weaken your resolve to fight temptation.

When my friend made his simple-life admission, he was saying something else to me. In a real way his poverty had protected him from being able to fully follow the trail of his greed. No, it didn't protect him from being envious and discontent at points, but he simply did not have the money to pay for what his selfish heart could imagine. This point is precisely why the Bible does alert us to the danger of riches. We come into this world as people who need to be retrained. We come into this world as a danger to ourselves. We are naturally more discontent than content. We are naturally attracted to what should scare us. We intuitively push against God's boundaries. So, anything in our lives that protects us from us, anything that restrains us, or anything that makes it hard for us to go where our desires are able to wander is a blessing.

In this way money is a danger. It takes off one restraint—affordability—and in so doing, exposes our hearts. It's only when God's grace has formed in us truly contented hearts that we can live retrained lives, not following the rabbit trail of every selfish desire that our wallets can afford. Look, most of us regularly buy what we do not need because we have followed desires that need to be restrained because we can afford whatever in that moment caught the attention of our hearts.

5) Money can finance your allegiance to the kingdom of self.

Well this is the bottom line. I've already said much about it, but this point too requires more special attention. There is no neutrality when it comes to your relationship to and daily use of money. As you hold and use your money, you must constantly remind yourself that the holding and using of money are acts of worship. That's just how significant this issue is. You are using your funds in the worship of yourself, even if you don't know it, or you are using your money in the self-conscious worship of God. You money is being invested in the building of your self-focused little kingdom of one or being offered in the interests of the grand and glorious eternal kingdom of God. This is the temptation that every sinner faces, to use the resources that he has been given to finance the wants, needs, and desires of the kingdom of self, and the more money that is in your hands, the more power this temptation tends to have.

So, money really does matter. You've been placed by God in a world where money exists and will influence the shape and direction of your life. Because money exposes you to both blessing and danger, your issues with money run at a deeper level than how much you understand finances and how well you have constructed your budget. Are both money, education, and budget beneficial? Of course! But they do not get down to the level where the real danger of money exists.

When I misuse money, I don't misuse it because I am ignorant or without a budget. No, I misuse it because at that point I don't care what God or anyone else says. I want what I want, and if I can use my resources to get it, I am going to get it. Money matters because it interacts with one of the most significant issues in my heart: the selfishness of sin. No amount of money, education, or budget construction has the power to free me from the ravenous greed of my sinful heart. For that, I can only look to one thing: the powerful grace of my Redeemer. He knows how selfish and greedy I can be. He knows how I make a resolution one day that I abandon the next. He knows how easily I am seduced into thinking that there is something in the creation that will satisfy my longing heart. He knows that I can say that I believe in God yet live as if he does not exist. So, he has blessed me with his right-here, right-now grace. Yes, that grace forgives me, but it does more: it provides everything I need to live in the money crazy world in the way that I was designed to live. What is the sweetest gift of that grace? Well, the sweetest gift is not a thing; it is a person. God's best gift is himself. He comes and lives inside of me so that when desire within meets temptation without, I will have just what I need to fight the battle. Money matters, but God's grace matters even more. It alone provides both the strength and the freedom you will continue to need until the dangers of money are no more.

11

TREASURE HUNTERS

From a distance he was a very, very successful man. From humble roots he had clawed his way to the top. As a high school and then college athlete he was as good as they get. Getting injured in his senior year was a setback, but with him no set back lasted for long. He was an academic star in his MBA program and was destined to do well in business. "Do well" turned out to be an inadequate description for the level of success he achieved at the speed at which he achieved it. The only reason he was not promoted faster was that his corporate mentors reasoned he was too young to be in charge. But he soon was in charge—in charge of everything he touched. He moved from corporation to corporation, climbing his way to the top. He was not about to let anything stop him. He would give more, work harder, arrive earlier, and stay later than anyone around him. He worked on weekends when everyone else was off. He took weekend-only vacations when he was allotted an entire month. He worked from home on holidays. He took work with him wherever he went. He was focused and determined.

He told me that at about fifteen years old he had hit what he called the "poverty wall." He was tired of watching his parents struggle. He was tired of cheap clothes and bad food. He was tired of being too embarrassed to bring anyone home. He was tired of the embarrassment of never having any money in his pocket. He remembers the morning very clearly when he told himself he was going to do everything he could to make money, lots of money. He would be rich if it killed him and he would enjoy everything rich guys enjoy. And when he looked back he said, "Everything I did had dollars in view."

He had made it. He had fulfilled his dream. He had the huge house, the luxurious cars, and the big boat. He wore fine suits and starched, monogrammed shirts. He was a member of several elite clubs. He was economically and politically powerful, and he loved it. He called himself a Christian, but you would never have known it. His Christianity was squeezed to the distant borders of his focused and busy life. In terms of the way he made decisions and invested his time and energy, his faith simply didn't matter. He knew what he wanted, and he gave his whole self to getting it, to maintaining it, to keeping it, and to enjoying it. The man had values, just not the right ones.

You've probably already figured it out. This man's money success was in reality a sad money mess. His marriage had crumbled under the debilitating weight of his drive and neglect. His wife was deeply hurt by the evidence that she had competed all these years with a mistress; that mistress was work. She was tired of the patience he exhibited in running commercial projects, while at home he was constantly impatient and quickly irritated. She felt she couldn't face any more years of being married but essentially living alone. Now that his kids were beginning to grow up, they had little time for him. They never had his attention, he didn't take the time to get to know them, and they weren't interested in a relationship with him. The tensions at home were huge, and the tensions on holidays were unbearable.

It took his wife moving out before he had any idea that something was wrong, and when he called his oldest son to talk about it, his son said, "Why are you surprised? She's hated you for years, and so do I," and he hung up on him. He was now harvesting the fruit of his own values, and so will you and I.

In a pointed moment of practical teaching, Jesus says in Matthew 6:19–33 that we are all treasure hunters. We name things as important to us, and we all live to get and experience what we have named as important. We all chase some golden dream. Our choices and actions are purposeful. There are things that we treasure and things that we don't. There are things that we become convinced we must have. There are treasures we have acquired and horde, and there are treasures we are yet working to get. And our lives follow the trail of choices, decisions, and actions that have been magnetized by what we hold dear.

In ways of which most of us are daily unaware, we tell ourselves that if we are able to possess and experience what we have come to treasure, then we will be satisfied and happy and finally experience that inner rest that every human being desires. We all live "If only I had _____" lives. It really is true: whatever sits on the other side of your "if only" is what you truly treasure. So, what do you treasure? How does it shape the way you assess your life, look at yourself, relate to others, think about God, and the make little and big decisions that everyone has to make? In short, what in the world are you really living for? Whatever it is you are living for is your functional treasure, no matter what you profess to believe and who you confess to serve.

But Christ doesn't leave the conversation there. He talks about your eyes. At first it seems to be an out of place observation, but it is germane. Every person is in possession of two systems of vision. When the typical person thinks of seeing, he thinks of his physical eyes. While the physical eyes are very important, and being physically blind is a dramatic deficiency, the physical eyes are not the most important vision system that you and I possess. We all have another set of eyes—the eyes of the heart. This set of eyes is your most important vision system. You can be physically blind and yet live quite well, but if the eyes of your heart are not working well, you won't live as you were designed to live.

The eyes of your heart are always envisioning something.

They are always fixed and focused on some hope, some dream, something of value that you are after. What the eyes of your heart envision will shape what your physical eyes look for and notice. Your physical vision is not neutral. No, it is guided by the eyes of your heart. You've experienced this. You go out and buy a new Nissan; you're so excited about your new car. But over the next few days something strange happens. You begin to see Nissans everywhere. It's as if everyone in the city where you live went out and bought a Nissan when you did. Now, you know that didn't happen. What has happened is that your excitement of heart at getting something you've wanted has changed the way you view your surroundings. Your functional values have altered the ways you see things. So, you notice Nissans like you didn't before and wrongly conclude that there are more of them than before, when actually they've been there before.

What for you is the treasure dream that shapes the way you see your world? What physical things get your focus because they connect to the treasure that has already commanded the focus of your heart? What are your physical eyes looking at that your heart has already been longing for? How has your way of seeing your world caused you to be discontent, driven, or envious? What things do your eyes notice because you heart has named them as important? The treasures of your heart will always shape the way you see.

Then Christ drops the bomb of his discussion of treasure with these words: "No one can serve two masters, for either he will hate the one and love the other, or he will be devoted to the one and despise the other. You cannot serve God and money" (Matt. 6:24) In these words Jesus is alerting us to how high the stakes are and to what it is that he is really talking about. What are the stakes of his treasure conversation? Why is this conversation so powerfully important? Why should each of us look at ourselves in the mirror of these words? The answer is clear: because we will surrender our heart to some kind of master. No one will escape. No heart will live free. Everyone's heart is mastered by something, and what masters your heart will shape your thoughts, desires, choices, words, actions, and emotions. There is simply no conversation more important than this. Human beings were created to live under mastery, and we all do. The only question is, what master?

Then Jesus reveals what this conversation is really about. It's about a great spiritual war that somehow, someway, is fought on the battlefield of the heart of every human being. It is the battle between two kings who seek to defend and expand their kingdoms. It is a war that no one will escape and will leave a whole lot of carnage. It's the great conflict between King Christ and King Money. One of these kings will become the functional master of your heart. One of these kings will guide your decisions. Each of these kings offers you hope, life, and peace, but only one of these kings is able to deliver. Both of these kings will tell you how to view life and what is important to focus on as you do. And the reality is that your heart simply isn't able to love them both, and in your life you just aren't able to serve them both. If you love one, you will end up hating the other, and if you serve one, you will end up ignoring the other. It is a great spiritual reality that just doesn't get enough play in the church of Jesus Christ.

It should get your notice that of all the false masters, all the pseudo-kings that Jesus could warn you about, he chooses money. Could it be that Jesus understands that this false king is the most seductive and deceptive of them all? Could it be that this is the master whose power it is hardest for us to escape? Could it be that nothing besides money more forcefully challenges the mastery of Jesus over your heart? Could it be that for people who are hardwired to live for treasure, the treasure nature of money makes it particularly hard to resist? Could it be that Christ is alerting us to the fact that many more of us bow at the feet of this king than we tend to think? Could it be that this cruel king has left a much bigger trail of carnage in our lives and relationships than we have tended to think? With a few simple words Christ drops a bomb in the middle of our comfortable and self-satisfied lives.

Perhaps many of us are confused as to who the master is that we are really serving. Maybe we haven't surrendered to the lordship of Jesus Christ after all. Perhaps we give lip service to the King of kings while in our daily lives we do homage to the Money King. Perhaps the degree of our drive, discontent, and debt exposes the king we are really serving. Perhaps what many of us attempt to do on Sunday is switch kings, because the King we have come into the room to worship is not actually the king we have been serving all week. If your week is spent loading up more debt on credit cards that you don't know how you'll pay so that you can have more physical stuff, you have worshiped at the feet of King Money. If you have to farm out your children to some care provider because you and your spouse have to work to maintain the upper-middle-class lifestyle that you think you cannot live without, you have worshiped King Money all week. If you work more than you should work to acquire more wealth and power, you are worshiping King Money. If your security is found in how much money is in your bank account, how nice your house is, and how hot your car is, you are doing homage to King Money. If you have sleepless nights wondering how you're going to pay the minimum monthly payment on several credit cards, you have offered your heart to King Money. If you get more personal excitement shopping than you do attending your church's worship service, maybe the mall is your temple, and perhaps money really is the king you serve.

The issue that Christ drops in the middle of his teaching is this: either you are investing your life in the pursuit of money and what it will get you, or you are investing your life in pursuit of God and what he says is of value. Either you are working to fund the success of your kingdom, or you are giving yourself in service of the kingdom of God. At street level either you are wor-

shiping King Christ and giving yourself to what he says is important, or you are worshiping King Money and giving yourself to
the pursuit of money and the comfort, pleasure, possessions, and
power it can buy. There really is no neutral ground. It is true that
everyone's life is organized by the functional worship of one of
these kings. Remember, we're all just a gang of treasure hunters;
we're all after what we've named as important. The only thing
that distinguishes us is the kind of treasure we live in pursuit of.

Jesus concludes this passage, saying: "Seek first the kingdom
of God and his righteousness and all these things will be added
to you" (Matt. 6:33). But this is not the only place in the Bible
where this convicting conversation takes place. Consider these
passages also:

> Jesus said to him, "If you would be perfect, go, sell what you
> possess and give to the poor, and you will have treasure in
> heaven; and come, follow me." (Matt. 19:21)

> But woe to you who are rich, for you have received your con-
> solation. (Luke 6:24)

> And he said to them, "Take care, and be on your guard against
> all covetousness, for one's life does not consist in the abundance
> of his possessions." (Luke 12:15)

> But God said to him, "Fool! This night your soul is required of
> you, and the things you have prepared, whose will they be?
> So is the one who lays up treasure for himself and is not rich
> toward God." (Luke 12:20–21)

> Fear not, little flock, for it is the Father's good pleasure to give
> you the kingdom. Sell your possessions, and give to the needy.
> Provide yourselves with moneybags that do not grow old, with
> a treasure in the heavens that does not fail, where no thief ap-
> proaches and no moth destroys. (Luke 12:32–33)

> Jesus, seeing that he had become sad, said, "How difficult it is
> for those with wealth to enter the kingdom of God! For it is

easier for a camel to go through the eye of a needle than for a rich person to enter the kingdom of God." (Luke 18:24–25)

All of these passages speak to the great inescapable conflict between God the King and King Money. All address the power of money to tempt and ultimately control us. Because you live in a physical world, filled with interesting and beautiful physical things that can be acquired through the possession of physical money, it is easy to be distracted, side-tracked, deceived, seduced, derailed, and kidnapped. Now, I want to make this clear: the Bible never teaches that the physical world and all the beautiful things in it are evil. The Bible never says it is evil to find pleasure in created things. The Bible never says it is wrong to own some of them. The Bible never says that money is evil. It never teaches that it is evil to acquire it or spend it. It never teaches that all rich people are unspiritual and all poor people are godly. You don't solve the battle with King Money by cursing money or physical things, because the battle is really a battle for your heart.

What the Bible clearly teaches is that when functional, life-shaping love for money and what it allows you to acquire and enjoy squeezes out of your heart the functional, life-shaping love for God that was designed to be the organizing principle of your life, then you are a person in deep spiritual trouble. Money is not evil, but it makes a very, very bad god. Wealth is not evil in itself, but you must not let it rule your heart. Money is one of God's good creations, but this good thing becomes a bad thing for you when it becomes a ruling thing. You simply cannot serve the King of kings and have acquisition of wealth as the organizing dream of your heart. You must not love the creation more than you love the Creator; so you cannot have money as the treasure you crave and at the same time tell yourself that you are living to gain the eternal treasures of the kingdom of God.

But I'm afraid this is what many of us are doing. We don't seem to be aware of the contradiction inherent in the way we live. We don't seem to be aware that money and things are the distributors of our joy. We don't seem to realize how much of our time and energy is spent gaining, maintaining, protecting, repairing, and enjoying the physical stuff of this earth. We don't seem to grasp how many hopes and dreams, sadnesses, and disappointments are attached to money and things. We fail to see how much we struggle with greed, entitlement, envy, and covetousness. We don't see how much the lack of money or the desired thing causes us to doubt the goodness of God. And because we don't see all this, we don't realize how, as we gather for corporate worship, we essentially have to switch kings, because the King we have come to worship is not the king we have served all week. It is a spiritual bomb dropped in the middle of our comfortable materialistic lives. It's the bottom line: "You cannot serve God and money." There is no compromise and there is no room for making deals. The exclusivity of Christ's statement should be a source of conviction to us all. It surely gives me pause, even as I write these words.

THE DANGER OF PLAYING WITH THE BOX

He frustrated me, but he didn't know it, and he surely didn't mean it. My son didn't get into gifts. It would be Christmas or his birthday, and we would put a well-wrapped gift in front of him, and he would discard what we had bought him and with great delight would play with the box. It happened enough times that on a particular Christmas I was determined I would keep shopping until I fought a toy that I knew he would be attracted to and actually occupy himself with.

Staying out shopping longer than we should have, Luella and I finally found the gift. We just knew it was made for him, and we were convinced he would love it. When it came time for him to open that gift, we were very excited, much more than he was. He tore into the box, took out the toy, and actually began to play with it. I couldn't believe it—finally!

I went into the kitchen to get something to drink, got engaged in a conversation, and after a few minutes went back into the living room where he was, and he was sitting in the box!

Now, maybe you're wondering why I am telling you this story in the midst of our consideration of the fact that we are all treasure hunters who daily deal with the battle between King Christ and King Money. Well, I think many of us are like my son. We have been given a wonderful gift. In fact, "wonderful" is a woefully inadequate word to describe it. It is the ultimate gift, the gift of gifts, the best gift that could ever be given. It is absolutely gorgeous from every perspective. It is the one gift that every human being who has ever taken a breath desperately needs, whether they know it or not. It is the only gift that is truly essential for life. It is a gift that you could never earn, achieve, or deserve. It is the only gift that has the power to change you and everything about you. It is not a gift you can purchase; it is only ever given. If you don't want this gift, you should, and if you don't think you need this gift, you do.

What is it? It is the gift of the grace of the Lord Jesus Christ. Yet I am afraid that in the face of being given this awesome, life-changing gift, many of us are content to play with the box. We're content with a little bit of biblical literacy. We're content with a bit of theological knowledge. We're content with occasional moments of ministry. We're content to put a little money in the offering plate. We're content with a casual relationship to our small group. We're content with a Christianity that lives best on Sunday morning. We've been given the best of gifts, but we're quite satisfied with playing with the box. We're not holding onto the gift of grace with both hands and a thankful heart. We're not saying, "I can't believe I was given this gift. I'm not letting go of this gift until it has done everything it was meant to do for me. I want to be wherever this gift is valued, explained, and encouraged. I am willing to surrender whatever is necessary to pursue what this gift can do for me and through me for others. And I will give myself to the worship of the One who so graciously did what was necessary so that this gift would be mine."

No, sadly many of us play with the box, and we do because there is something else that has eaten up the love of our hearts. There is something else that we daily serve. There is something else that has captured our hopes and dreams. Yes, we're thankful that we have been saved, and we probably won't stop going to church anytime soon, but something else organizes our lives and has captured our imagination. King Money has whispered big promises in our ears, and we have believed his lies. And we live in hot pursuit of what he has no right to promise and no power to deliver—life. So, in our lack of fulfillment, we keep spending more to acquire more, but it doesn't work. The buzz doesn't last very long; before long the emptiness of dissatisfaction returns, so we go out there hoping that this time King Money will deliver. He can't and he won't, so what we're left with is empty hearts and empty wallets. Our income chases our lifestyle. It is insanity. The lasting legacy is debt, and for many of us, the way with debt is to spend more.

We don't have a budget problem; we have a treasure problem. We don't have a financial problem; we have a kingship problem. We don't have a *things* problem; we have a heart problem. If we don't deal with the kingship problem, we will never successfully deal with the spending and budget problems that so many of us face.

YOUR BUDGET AND GOD'S GRACE

Two of Christ's most striking parables say it all. They get to the deepest level of how human beings were hardwired and how we daily function. They may be two of the briefest of all the parables, but their brevity should not condition our evaluation of their importance. They expose the deepest struggle of our hearts and by so doing point to how fundamental our need for grace is.

> The kingdom of heaven is like the treasure hidden in a field, which a man found and covered up. Then in his joy he goes and sells all that he has and buys that field. Again, the kingdom

of heaven is like a merchant in search of fine pearls, who, on finding one pearl of great value, went and sold all that he had and bought it. (Matt. 13:44–46)

What are these two little parables about? What do they confront us with? Their one central message is the incalculable value of the kingdom of God. What is this kingdom? It is God's gracious plan of redemption for us and the world we live in. What is the treasure of great value, the pearl of great price? It is Christ himself and his gift of forgiving, rescuing, transforming, and delivering grace. And what the parables argue is that there is nothing more valuable than God's gift of his Son of grace, and there is nothing more worth celebrating than the redemption that comes with that grace. And the parables demonstrate that if you properly value this treasure/pearl it will radically alter the choices you make and the actions you take in your everyday life.

You cannot properly value this kingdom and go on with the self-centered, money-driven, and thing-oriented way of living that is normal for most people. You can't properly value grace and have your celebration of a pursuit of that grace be relegated to the time left in a schedule that is fully booked in pursuit of another kingdom. If you value this treasure properly, it will become the organizing value of your life. It will determine how your time, energy, and money are spent. It will rearrange your schedule. It will form a new way of thinking about your budget. It will shape your relationships and your leisure. It will reform your relationship to your church. It will fill your heart with joy as it turns your life upside down.

But I will make this confession, and perhaps you should too: I don't always properly value the treasure that is Jesus and his grace. To my grief, I am still in possession of a fickle heart. My heart wanders, and because it does my eyes and my wallet do too. I spend money on things I don't really need. I envy what others have that I would like to possess. Maybe my low-grade discontent is the giveaway. There are moments when I am not satisfied, and I simply want more, even though I already have much, much more than I need.

Immanuel has invaded my life by his grace. He has done for me what I could not do for myself. His grace has provided the rescue that the law could not provide. He has lavished on me love that I could never in my most delusional moment think that I deserve. He does not turn his back to me even in my most arrogant and rebellious moments. He never mocks my weaknesses or throws my sin back in my face. He is faithful when I don't have the sense to be; he fights on my behalf even in the moments when I am too lazy to. And he will not quit doing all of these things in and for me until his work of grace is complete. The gift of this treasure to me is the stunning reality of my existence. The eternal significance of it defies the human vocabulary.

But I don't always see it that way. My heart still wanders. I am still in need of grace. My need of grace is so profound that I need grace in order to properly value the grace I need. Here's what is important about this: our problem with money doesn't begin with overvaluing the physical created world. No, our problem with money is rooted in a dramatic undervaluing of the gift of Jesus and his grace. It is only when King Christ is given the proper value in our hearts that King Money will have neither the power nor the room to rule us. It seems that often in the churches' money discussions we forget this, and because we do, we ask the law to do what only grace can accomplish. A budget can expose what your heart truly values, but a budget has no power to make you worship the right king. A budget can give you useful spending guidelines, but it has no power to restrain your fickle and wandering heart. A budget can make you more money aware, but it will not deliver you from temptation.

So we once again confess our disloyalty to the King of kings, we pray for strength to fight the Money King, and we rest in the knowledge that God's grace is sufficient even in our moments of greatest weakness. We know we will fail again, give way to temptation again, and worship the wrong king again, and when we do, we know we will be greeted with that valuable grace once again. So, we get up tomorrow to fight the war again, knowing we are not alone and that our King will never turn a deaf ear to the needy cries of his people.

12

MONEY IS NOT THE PROBLEM—LOVE IS

They were living under crushing debt. It was all so complicated that that day in my office when they finished telling me their story, I didn't know what to say. They were the living familial case study of what the love of money looks like. Both husband and wife had been married before, so theirs was a blended family. They had together raised materialistic, entitled, and demanding children. It's no wonder they had, because they both thought they deserved the "good life" and were quite willing to spend to get it. And spend they did! There seemed to be no end to their cycle of desire, expenditure, possession, debt, dissatisfaction. They loved money for how it made them feel. They loved money for what it could get them. They loved money for how it made them look in the eyes of others. They loved money for its power. They loved money because they thought it meant God loved them. They loved money for what it could buy them out of. They loved money!

When I met them, their house of self-oriented, materialistic dreams had begun to crash down. As I listened to their story, it became very clear to me that somewhere along the way they had gone money insane. They seemed almost incapable of holding onto their money. They invented ways of spending their next dollar even before it had been earned. Because it wasn't just goods and pleasure that were mounting up, but debt as well, they decided they had to do something. So they took out a second mortgage on their second home. Borrowing more to get out of debt was not a good solution in the first place, but guess what they did with their newfound thousands? They put it in their ATM account. Yes, you read it right. They mortgaged their house and used the proceeds to fund more reckless spending. In fact, in celebration of their new cash flow, the husband went out and bought his wife a $3,500 ring. They were money drunk, money addicted, and money mad, but they seemed not to know it.

Because of the pressures, the husband and wife were tense, irritable, and in almost constant conflict with one another. The children were in a constant contest to see who would end up with the biggest pile of stuff. They were demanding, complaining, and critical. The husband was spending less and less time at home because he couldn't deal with the conflict there, and the wife, feeling abandoned, began to think about how to get out of her marriage. With all the division, the semblance of an intentional spiritual life went out the window. God had long since been replaced as the object of their street-level worship. Church was no longer on the weekly calendar, and giving to God's work, well, there simply wasn't enough money for that. For them, the love of money was rapidly becoming the source of all kinds of evil.

HOW IS LOVE OF MONEY THE ROOT OF EVIL?

When you first read it, it doesn't seem that it could be true. It seems as if there are all kinds of things that are more evil then loving money. And it doesn't on the surface seem that loving money could lead you to all other kinds of evil. So it is important to take time to unpack the spiritual dynamics of the love of money. Let's examine 1 Timothy 6:6–10:

> Godliness with contentment is great gain, for we brought noth-
> ing into the world, and we cannot take anything out of the

world. But if we have food and clothing, with these we will be content. But those who desire to be rich fall into temptation, into a snare, into many senseless and harmful desires that plunge people into ruin and destruction. For the love of money is a root of all kinds of evils. It is through this craving that some have wandered away from the faith and pierced themselves with many pangs.

If you read those words carefully, you begin to get a clue that the love of money is connected to things that are significantly bigger than money. Consider the profound connections Paul makes in this provocative little passage. The love of money is fundamentally not an overspending problem; it is a *contentment* problem ("Godliness with contentment is great gain"). The love of money is also an *identity* problem (". . . for we brought nothing into this world"). The love of money is a *fallen world* problem (". . . fall into temptation"). And the love of money is a *worship* problem ("But those who desire to be rich . . ."). The root system of the love of money runs deeper and wider through the soil of the human heart than we tend to think.

Paul begins his discussion with *contentment* because the roots of our problem with money are to be found there. Discontentment *is* the soil in which the love of money grows. I don't think that we value-rate discontentment properly. Discontentment seems like an inconsequential sin. For most of us, it means little more than we wish we had more, and in our complaining we're just not going to be the life of the party. But discontentment is much more spiritually significant and influential than that. What the discontented person lacks is something more fundamental and life-shaping than happiness; the discontented person lacks humility. He really does think of himself more highly than he ought to think. He really is convinced that he deserves what he doesn't actually deserve. He lives as though he is entitled to things to which he's not entitled, and because he feels entitled, he thinks it's his right to demand them. He can't handle the guy next to him having what he has been unable to acquire, and his discontentment will ultimately bring him to question the goodness of God. Discontentment is a very significant thing.

The lack of humility that fuels discontentment is about more than being a bit full of ourselves and bragging too much; it's about a heart that has been captured by self-glory. Its life has turned inward, when we have been created to live an upward (love God) and an outward (love neighbor) life. It really is making it all about us. It is a lifestyle that is shaped by the unholy self-love trinity: my wants, my needs, and my feelings. It is about making my personal definition of happiness the most important ethical commitment of my life. It does mean that my every day is spent in the pursuit of my pleasure, my comfort, and my ease. It is me in the center of my world. It is "I love me, and I have a wonderful plan for my life."

Because I am in the center of my world, and because that means that God isn't, money can't possibly be in its proper place. You see, if God is in the center of my world and I acknowledge that I was created to live for him, then I look to him to provide in his grace what I need to be what I'm supposed to be and to do what I was designed to do. But if I am at the center, if it really is all about me, then money can become my surrogate, my replacement savior. How, you may ask? Well, when my happiness is at the center and the Creator is out of the picture, then I will look to creation for my happiness. So money then becomes the savior that delivers all the things that I think will bring me joy. No longer living for God's glory but obsessed by my own, I daily ask money to save me from the want and discomfort that is the principle evil I work to avoid.

Would you not agree that living for self rather than living for God is at the core of all kinds of evil? Well, that is exactly what the love of money is all about. When I am in the center of my world and not God, I will live an entitled, self-focused, demanding life marked by the discontent that selfishness always produces. Self-glory is at the center of the original sin in the garden of Eden, and it is the soil in which all sin has grown ever since.

But there is more. The love of money is also an *identity* problem. The love of money is connected to forgetting who you are and what your life is about. Since you have been created for a life beyond this one, hardwired for forever, it makes no sense to view life as being all about the pleasures, possession, experiences, and power of the moment. It is true: you brought nothing in, and you'll take nothing out, and when you're making your exit, what you have amassed won't do much for you or mean much to you. If you forget who you are, if you deny what life is about, then it will be very hard to keep money in its proper place. You will love it, crave it, do everything you can to get it, envy the guy who has more of it, and judge the goodness of God by his willingness to deliver it. The love of money sits right in the middle of a lifestyle that forgets eternity, that lives selfishly, that prioritizes the present, and that is more focused on your physical comfort than on your eternal destiny. This right-here, right-now, "you only go around once" way of living is a vat of all kinds of evil. Much more will be said about eternity and your money in a chapter to come.

There is something else Paul wants you to know. The love of money is a *fallen world* problem. The love of money is such a significant and important issue because we live in a world that is not functioning as God intended, and because it isn't, it is a place where temptation is all around us. You cannot get up in the morning without being faced with devious, deceitful, and seductive temptations of some kind. Ten thousand voices whisper in your ear, each calling you away from the life God designed for you to live and enjoy. And what is the temptation that Paul talks about in Romans 1? It is not the temptation to replace worship and service of the Creator for worship and service of the creation. It is attaching our identity and our inner sense of well-being to something in the creation. It is asking the creation to give us what only the Creator can—life.

You see, ultimately the love of money is about *worship*. It connects us to the evil of evils, offering the love, adoration, worship, and service that we were meant to give to God and God alone to something in the world that he created. Because love of money sits at the dark intersection of love of self and worship of the creation, it doesn't lead us to keep the two great commandments, and because we don't, we will do many things that are evil in the sight of God.

The love of money is not a little thing; it really is a portal to all kinds of evil. Why? Because it connects us to foundational, life-shaping issues of the heart, such as contentment, identity, how we understand and relate to the world we live in, eternity, and worship. If we get these issues wrong, there is no way that we will live as God intended.

WHY LOVE OF MONEY MAKES YOU DANGEROUS TO YOU

If the terrible triad of love for self, worship of the creation, and love of money rules your heart, you will be a danger to yourself. It is only when you live for God that you have both the grace-given desire and the power to say no to yourself, to exercise daily self-control, and to live as God has called you to live. When you are in the center of your existence, why would you ever say no to you? Self-centered living curses authority, boundaries, rules, and restraint. There is only one rule for the truly self-oriented human being: "I will have what I will have." When you are the center, you will be the ultimate consumer. You will have ravenous, insatiable hunger. You will always be on the lookout for the next pleasure. You will constantly be moaning, "If only I had _____." The fact that you don't have everything you want will be the biggest grief of your life. When you love you, you'll love money because it allows you to indulge you. When you love you, you'll love money because it makes you feel better about you. When you love you, you'll love money because it alters how others look at you. When you love you, you'll love money because it can help you to depend only on you. When you love you, you'll love money because it keeps you from having to say no to you.

Saying no recognizes and submits to the fact that there is someone who rules all things, and it is not you. Saying no to yourself recognizes God's existence and submits to his commands. But when you are living for you, no matter what your formal confession is, you are living as if God doesn't exist and as if you have the right to write your own rules. The love of money sits at the epicenter of a lifestyle of self-glory and constant craving. It is not a lifestyle in which sin is restrained.

Here's the bottom line: in a way that is foundational and life-shaping, the love of money replaces love for God in your heart. That is disastrous enough, but not only does it replace God, but it also has no power to deliver the satisfaction that your heart seeks. So you have to go back again and again, craving more money, hoping more, spending more, and living from short-term buzz to short-term buzz, all the while becoming more addicted than you are aware of.

But there is even more. Because love of money pushes love for God out of your heart, it pushes you to the center of your life. No longer shaped by God's glory, God's will, God's plan, God's grace, and God's rules, your life is shaped by your cravings, your "needs," your plan, and your self-oriented rules. You simply cannot be in the center of your world and be your own highest authority and not be a moral danger to yourself, because when you are at the center you will not say no to you. That's what the love of money does to you; it draws you into a dangerous world of self-glory.

What does this "I am a danger to myself" lifestyle look like? Consider the four descriptions that follow.

1) "I deserve," unquestioned.

When love for God doesn't rule your heart, you're left alone at the center of your universe, and you think you deserve things that you do not deserve. You will pursue your own feelings of entitlement. You will not question your self-orientation. You will feel little guilt that you spend most of your time and money taking care of you. You will spend more time complaining than you do giving thanks. You will find it much harder to give than to take for yourself. You will see your money as belonging to you for your use. No matter how much money you have, you will tend to think that you deserve more. You won't see any level of personal affluence as a blessing but as your right, and you will spend so much time using your money to take care of you that you will have little time to look for ways to use it to bless and serve others.

2) "I want," unrestrained.

Rather than your life being shaped and directed by God's existence, his glory, his grace, and his moral call, it will be moved by your wants, your needs, and your feelings. You've seen it in your children or the children of others—we really can be an endless catalog of desires. From the moment of our birth, our capacity to desire is in need of redemption and restraint. You cannot live in the way you were created to live and have a lifestyle that chases personal desires. We all need something glorious and transcendent to capture and motivate our hearts. We all need to be rescued from ourselves by being spiritually awakened to something bigger than us. No life is more dangerous than the "me-ward" life that every sinner quests for.

The life that you were created to live is always shaped by saying no, not to God or others but to yourself. You want things that you do not need. You will crave things that you should not have. You will desire more than is necessary. You will be attracted to what is destructive. You will see as beautiful things that are ugly in God's sight. If you use your time, energy, and money to follow the trail of your desires, you will expose yourself to all kinds of evil and end up destroying your life.

3) "Me first," undebated.

I was racing toward the checkout line, looking left and right to see which line my fellow shoppers would choose. I was already irritated that someone was going to beat me to the counter and delay me a few minutes. Behind three people with multiple things to purchase, I was giving way to my irritated heart, when by grace, right there in the checkout line, God rescued me from me. I thought, "I have no right to be first. My schedule is not more important than theirs. God rules even these little moments for his glory and my good. Nothing significant is going to happen in the next three minutes." Grace gave me back my sanity again. The "me first," money-fueled mentality of self-glory is not only insane; it is the source of all kinds of evil. It reduces other human beings to obstacles in your way, questions the sovereignty and goodness of God, and tramples his call to love your neighbor as yourself.

4) "I will," unchallenged.

Perhaps "I will" is the ultimate danger of this way of living. It causes me to set myself up as king rather than to live as a willing and joyful slave of the King of kings. No longer do I pray, "Your kingdom come, your will be done on earth as it is in heaven." No, I want my kingdom to come. I secretly desire my will to be done right here, right now where I am living. I want control that I should not have. I want predictable days and an uninterrupted schedule. I want people to agree with me and submit to my plans. I want people to indulge my cravings and give way to my demands. I am living for myself, and I want you to live for me too. And my money becomes the currency that finances my self-directed little kingdom of one.

Because love of money pushes out love for God as the chief motivator of my heart, I won't just struggle with the proper use of money and the things it can buy; I will struggle with all kinds of other evils. You simply cannot have yourself at the center and not end up with a life that is evil in the eyes of God.

It is with sadness that I have written the last several pages, not because I don't love the wisdom of God's truth but because of how it exposes the sin, weakness, and failure of my own heart. I wish I could say that I am free of the struggles I have described, but I am not. This discussion of the dangers of the love of money has exposed my fickle, wandering heart. I am not free of craving what I do not need. I haven't been fully delivered from confusing need with selfish desire. I am still tempted to think of my resources as belonging to me for my use. I am not completely free of envying the ease or affluence of others. I still find places in my life where it is very difficult to say no to me. The treasures, pleasures, and comforts of this physical world are still too attractive to me. I know I still waste money in places where it could be used so much better. I know I can have enough and still tell myself that I need more. I know there are times when my kingdom is more precious to me than God's. There are moments when what God says is evil doesn't look so evil to me. I am not free from feeling the intoxicating excitement of money. I still have moments of dreaming of the luxuries that I would enjoy if piles of money were dropped on me out of the blue. I don't always buy because need has forced me to. I still waste money on pleasures that quickly fade. All of this means that I have discovered there is more love of money in my heart than I would have confessed before I began work on this book. And it is humbling to face the fact that right theology, biblical literacy, ministry calling, experience, and skill have not rescued me.

This piece of writing has exposed a spiritual schizophrenia in me that I suspect is in many of you. Perhaps your commitment to the ministry of your church and the discipline of regular giving has caused you to wrongly conclude that the love of money is not an issue for you. Perhaps your ability to keep yourself above the deep waters of debt has convinced you that the love of money is not a struggle for you. Perhaps comparing yourself to others who, from what you see, seem financially insane has made you think that when it comes to the love of money, you're okay. But I would ask you right here, right now, to put down this book and to stop, look, and listen. Examine your heart and your life. Is there evidence that perhaps when it comes to love of money you're not doing as well as you think you are? Could it be that there are subtle pockets of evil in your life that would not be there if God and money were in their proper place in your heart?

My spiritual schizophrenia and yours is an argument for our foundational need for grace. Since I am the thing of greatest danger to me, since my deepest problems reside not outside of me but literally in my heart, I cannot help myself. I cannot solve my problem. A better budget won't help me if something rules my heart other than God. Good financial counsel won't help me in the places where I am committed to building my own kingdom. I need to be rescued, restored, and empowered. I need to be liberated from my slavery to me. I need my desires to be refocused and redirected. I need to live with contentment in my heart. I need eyes to see the lavish blessings that greet me every day. I need to love God more fully and people more actively. I need grace!

God wrote the events and controlled the people and locations of history so that at the right moment Jesus would come, because there was no other hope for us. He lived the life we simply never could or would live. He willingly died the death that he did not deserve, but we did. He satisfied all the requirements of God's law and God's anger. He walked away from the grave, conquering death. It was all done so that in our rebellion, inability, and sin, we would have the help that we need in our time of need.

You see, you don't have to carry the heavy burden of money guilt and money shame around with you. You don't have to work to convince yourself or others that you are money wise or money righteous. You don't have to work to justify your self-oriented spending or your lack of compassion for others. You don't have to defend the choices you have made. You don't have to do any of this, because on the cross Jesus liberated you not only from the mess of your sin but also from the delusion of your righteousness. Because of what Jesus has done for you, because his righteousness covers you, in your darkest moment of failure you don't have to run from him. No, Jesus bore the full weight of your rejection in that moment on the cross when the Father turned his back on him. He willingly endured that rejection so that in your hour of need, you would never, ever see God turn his back on you.

You don't have to ask strategies, tactics, plans, and rules to be your savior, because you have a Savior who is with you, in you, and for you. He is your life, and his grace is your hope. Run to him, as I have been doing, for the forgiveness and rescue that only he can give.

THE GLORY OF GOD AND MONEY

The beauty of grace is that it not only rescues me; it puts me in my place. Grace humbles me as it opens my eyes to the fact that it is not all about me. Grace causes me to love the King rather than wanting to be the king. Grace exposes how messed up and spiritually needy I actually am. Grace welcomes me to a kingdom much bigger and more beautiful than my own. Grace enables me to invest in eternal things rather than all the temporary pleasures that could consume all my time and money. Grace makes me feel small without feeling alone and unloved. Grace tells me I'm poor while offering me greater riches than I have ever known. Grace keeps letting me know the danger I am to myself and the depth of my moment-by-moment need. Grace reveals how fickle my heart is without ever ridiculing my weakness. Grace doesn't just humble me once, but again and again as my proud heart inserts me in the center again.

Only grace can cause things to grow in your heart that will progressively liberate you from your bondage to the love of money or any other thing that would challenge the rule that God alone should have. Only grace can turn an entitled person into a *thankful* one. Only grace can transform a demanding and envious heart into one that is truly *content*. It is grace alone that can cause you to be *patient*, free from a heart that wants what it wants right now. Only grace can enable you to be *compassionate*, able to see and care about the needs of others instead of being so dominated by your own. And it is grace alone that can turn this pseudo-king into one who invests his time and money into the *service* of the King.

Thankfulness, contentment, patience, compassion, service— five ingredients of the heart of one who no longer worships at the feet of the Money King but has been welcomed and empowered by grace into the service of the one true King. Do these things reside in my heart? In yours? The answer for all of us is, in bits and pieces they do. But the battle goes on. We will once again lose our way. There will be moments that are animated by loving money and forgetting God. There will be times when the glory of what we want will be more important to us than the glory that is God's due. We will once again spend what we don't have, to acquire what doesn't satisfy. We will waste dollars and cry out that we're needy.

But grace won't leave us to ourselves. It won't give up and give us over to our own devices. Grace will expose us once again. It will convict us once again. It will forgive us once again. It will empower us once again. It will wrap arms of divine love around us once again, and we will remember who we are and what we have been given. And by grace we will take one more step toward becoming the thankful and contented people that grace promises one day we will be.

13

YOU CAN'T TAKE
IT WITH YOU

It is one of the most radical concepts that Scripture presents. It is counterintuitive, defying both our physical assumptions and philosophical logic. Even for most people who trust the teaching of the Bible, it isn't embraced and understood in a way that shapes their daily choices, decisions, and actions. Its right-here, right-now implications will cause you to live in a different way in every area of your life. You cannot live properly without this in view. In fact the Bible teaches that this reality is hardwired in the heart of every human being. Without this perspective, biblical faith makes no sense at all. It is an essential ingredient to the plan of God. You long for it even if you don't know you do. The sadly broken world around you groans for it.

What is this essential and radical perspective? *Eternity*. The Bible clearly teaches that this life is not all there is. It is the fact that every human being is heading for a forever of some kind. What does this have to do with you and your money? The answer is, everything. You simply cannot understand and live out of God's plan for you and your money if you are not living with eternity in view. I am persuaded that much of the money insanity that lives in us and around us is the direct and practical result of culturally endemic *eternity amnesia*. So I want to consider the implications of your belief in forever on the way you think about and handle the financial resources that God has entrusted to you to steward.

What has gripped most of us and the culture around us is what I call *practical me-istic presentism*. It's *practical* because it really does shape our daily living. It's *me-istic* because it puts us and our personal wants, needs, feeling, hopes, and dreams in the center of our field of concern. It's a fundamentally me-centered way of thinking about life. And it's *present-ism* because it's all about this moment. In other words, it's fueled by a short-term view of life rather than the long-view perspective that dyes all that the Bible teaches. This practical me-istic present-ism (PMP) is a critical causal ingredient in money insanity.

Let's begin by unpacking three tragic errors inherent in the PMP worldview, which characterizes many more of us than we tend to think.

1) It acts as if this moment is all there is.

Although we covered this error earlier, when we considered its impact on how we handle sex, it's worth covering again here in our discussion about money. This really is how most people live. They live as if the moment they're in isn't connected to anything bigger, as if life isn't going anywhere. When this is your street-level mentality, you load all of your fears, dreams, hopes, problem, and solutions into the here and now. Everything must happen, must be experienced, must be possessed, or must be solved right here, right now. It is a foundationally impatient way of living. You and I simply weren't designed to live this way. Ecclesiastes 3:11 says that God has "set eternity in the hearts of men." This means that in the heart of everyone is a longing for paradise. The world was designed such that life would give way to life, giving way to life, on into eternity. We were created for long living not short living. We were made to live with the consciousness that our existence is part of something bigger and that our lives extend beyond this present physical reality.

Forgetting this never leads anywhere good. It produces fear, that primal, unspoken fear that somehow, someway, life will pass us by. It's the fear that we won't possess or experience all that's possible. It's the dread that we will die with regret. This fear is accompanied by an anxiety that constantly asks, "What if I _____?" or "What if I don't _____?" It's what fills your mind as you're trying to go to sleep, but your mind is scanning your life, asking questions you can't really answer.

It is the opposite of a restful, patient, and contented way of living. It thinks more about what you don't have than what you've been blessed with. It scans the life of others to see if they have what you don't. It's a way of living shaped more by a cost-benefit analysis than by overarching moral commitments.

The fear, anxiety, and drive of this PMP are strengthened by a fourth thing: doubting God. If you don't understand or are not living in light of God's plan, you will tend to doubt his goodness. If you mistakenly think that the blessings he has promised must be received and enjoyed in the present moment, if you mistakenly think of now as a destination rather than as a preparation for a final destination yet to come, you will begin to wonder if God is there or if he cares or if he has the desire and power to do what he has promised. If you measure the goodness of God by the amount of paradise he has presently delivered to you, you will come to doubt his goodness. And when you doubt the goodness of God, you quit believing what he says, and you quit going to him for help. You simply don't entrust your life to someone you have come to doubt.

Need I say that all of this results in a money mess? If you are living as an eternity amnesiac you will spend too much, and what you spend, you will spend unwisely. If you forget that your life is connected to things much bigger than you and much longer than your physical days, you will spend your money in ways that are materialistic and selfish. If you forget who you are and what life is about, you will spend for short-term pleasure and comfort rather than for eternal gain. If you forget God's eternal plan, you will try to quiet your inner longings with material possessions and experiences.

Money sanity is only ever found in the context of living with eternity in view and trusting your life into the care of the One who understands and rules everything from eternity past to eternity future. Money sanity is found only when you rest in God's wisdom, faithfulness, timing, presence, and provision. If you don't trust God in this way, you will look to money to be your savior and to deliver to you things that it never can, because they are the gifts of him and him alone. In a vain quest, you will tend to spend more than you have on what will not deliver what you're seeking.

2) It thinks that material things can satisfy.

If you think that life is only about this present material existence, then it would make sense to think that material things really do have the power to satisfy your heart. As I have written before, the material world was not created to give your heart peace. The material world was designed to be one big finger that points you to the place where you heart will only ever find its peace and rest. The fulfillment that the glories of the physical creation give you is temporary at best. Jesus hints at this when he tells us that the earth-bound treasures that so many of us live for are temporary. He reminds us that thieves steal them, moths eat them, and rust destroys them. Why does he point this out? Because he wants us to know that they have no ability whatsoever to gives the lasting and eternal joy, hope, peace, satisfaction, and rest that we all seek.

The lie of lies in the Garden of Eden in that tragic moment of temptation is that life can be found somewhere outside of the Creator and his grace. The real life doesn't actually consist in what you have done, what you have acquired, or what you have experienced. Real life is only ever experienced in relationship with the One who is life and who alone has the power to offer life to all who entrust themselves to him.

So we unwisely spend time telling ourselves that this next thing, this next location, this next experience will satisfy us. It's the "If only I had . . ." way of living. But our pile of possessions sits as a monument to our discontent. Our experiences tell the story of our dissatisfaction. Our locations are the stops along the way of a journey that has not ended well. In a shocking materialism we have tried to buy life and it has not worked. It has left us fat, addicted, in debt, and discouraged, but still hoping that life can be bought in this material world somehow, someway. Let me interject here, that this is the functional lifestyle of many of us who hold onto a theological belief in eternity. We live with a fundamental disconnect between what we say we believe and how we live our lives.

3) It hopes that paradise is achievable now.

If the hunger for paradise is wired into your heart (and it is), either you will realize that this present life has been designed as a preparation for the paradise to come, or you will do your best and work your hardest to turn the present moment into the paradise it will never be. You and I live in a broken world that right now will not be the paradise we seek. You and I are flawed people, living with flawed people, and collectively we have no ability whatsoever to deliver paradise to one another. Every place you go and every created thing you handle has been damaged by the fall. This simply is not and won't be the paradise you seek. For all who have placed their trust in the Savior, paradise is a secure reality. The paradise for which your heart longs is coming, but you will not experience it right here, right now.

No, God has chosen to keep you in this broken world in order to use its brokenness to prepare you for what is to come. The brokenness you live in the middle of, and the difficulties you face there, are not in the way of God's good plan for you;

they are an important ingredient in it. Right now, God is not so much working to change your surroundings but to change you so that you are ready for the new surroundings he has planned and purchased for you in his grace.

Simply said, either you are waiting by faith for the paradise to come, or you are working with your hands to build paradise in the here and now. Looking for paradise in the here and now is another ingredient of the money madness inside many of us and has overtaken the culture around us. We frenetically spend on material things, physical experiences, and new locations in the search of a piece of paradise. Our hearts long for the freedom from external difficulty and internal emptiness that we so often feel. We instinctively know that there must be more, that this can't be it. Deep within us we feel like we're missing something. So in our eternity amnesia we don't lift up our eyes to look afar and consider the glories that are coming. No, we open our wallets and look around at what may have the potential to give us the paradise we are seeking. And because nothing can deliver it, we spend from thing to thing to thing, hoping that the next thing will deliver. But we don't end up with paradise. We end up with houses that are bigger and more luxurious than we need, cars that are more identity markers than means of transportation, a pile of possessions, many of which lie unused, amassed debt, and wallets that are empty. But the paradise that we've spent to get has eluded us. Sure, budgets are helpful, but only if they are a piece of handling our money with eternity in view.

When it comes to money, the PMP that lives inside us and that has captured our culture just cannot work. It will cause you to spend too much, it will tempt you to spend unwisely, and for all of your investment, it will leave you empty in the end.

HOW ETERNITY HELPS FREE YOU FROM MONEY INSANITY

We all have a disconnect in our lives. It surely is easier to conceptually embrace an area of biblical truth than to live in light of it.

None of us lives perfectly in light of all that the Bible teaches. We all sort of know that the purpose of the theology of Scripture is not just to help us check marks in all the right belief boxes. The Bible has a deeper, more personal agenda. It's that people intent on worshiping themselves and looking to creation for salvation would, by grace, become people who worship the Creator and live out of the belief that life can only ever be found in him.

Scripture is meant to transform you, and in transforming you to radically alter the way you live. None of us is perfectly there yet, and, thankfully, God greets our inconsistencies with patient grace. You see that grace offered to all of the inconsistent believers on the pages of Scripture. The only perfect hero of the Bible is the Lord himself! Yet we should quest by grace to live with greater consistency and joy in light of the mercies that have been lavished on us.

So it is with eternity. It surely is a whole lot easier to say we believe in forever than to live in the middle of implications of that reality. I had that box checked for years before I began to think about the right-here, right-now meaning of what I had intellectually assented to. I lived with no understanding of how this truth could liberate and protect me in very concrete ways. God's truth itself is a grace, used by God to protect us from us and from the temptations of a world gone bad. So I want to track for you how God intends the truth of eternity to come to protect you from money insanity. The following points are meant to prime the pump and get you thinking.

1) The existence of eternity immediately tells me that I have been designed for an existence with fundamentally bigger concerns than a right-here, right-now focus on my wants, my needs, my feelings.

Money insanity has its roots in the soil of the selfishness of sin. When I am in the center of my world, and my care for me dominates my thinking, deciding, and acting, there is no way I will use money as it was intended to be used. The existence of eternity tells me there is someone in charge who has put a plan into motion. I am not in charge, and my life does not belong to me. So it makes no sense to live as if my needs and concerns are all that matters. An acknowledgment of the reality of eternity can free me from the "my money belongs to me to better my life and to make me happy" view that we all tend to fall into.

Why do we get excited when we get a raise or a big tax rebate? We probably get excited because we have already thought of ways that money can help us possess or experience things that will make us happy. Eternity confronts us with the bigness, the grandeur, of life and the glory of the One who rules over it. In light of this, it's a bit insane to practically have no bigger purpose for our money than to buy our way out of need and to purchase what would satisfy our desires. If our life is meant to be connected to bigger things, then our money should be invested in things bigger as well. Our money has a bigger purpose than just being God's means of providing for us. *Is your use of money essentially self-oriented?*

2) The existence of eternity tells me that since this is not a destination but a preparation for a final destination, the goal of this moment is not to use my resources to turn now into as much of a paradise as I can afford.

The reality of eternity also confronts the destination mentality that shapes the living of so many of us. If this is all there is, if it's our final destination, then the goal really is to grab all the comfort and pleasure we can get our hands on. No eternity? It would make sense then to expend all our resources on making our life as enjoyable as we can. It's rather like the guy who is asked what he wants for his last meal. Seldom do people ask for brown rice and broccoli, because if it's your last meal you're not thinking what would be the healthiest choice. No, you're thinking, "If this is it, I'm going to have the most pleasurable meal possible, no matter how unhealthy it might be."

But this is not a destination. This moment is designed by God as a preparation for a final destination. By means of his faithful and often uncomfortable grace, God is preparing me for the eternity that grace has prepared for me. The money insanity that still lives in us and around us tends to treat the present moment as a destination and tends to ask again and again, "How can I make now more comfortable for me?" The goal of every moment is more than personal happiness. It is growth in holiness. What would it look like to spend your money with that in view? *Is your money use shaped by a destination or a preparation mentality?*

3) The existence of eternity tells me where and
when my only true satisfaction will be found.

Eternity is gloriously satisfying because God is in the middle of it. The existence of eternity confronts the insanity that fuels so much of our spending. What is this insanity? I have addressed it throughout this book and in the description of PMP earlier in this chapter, but it is such a huge issue that it bears repeating. It is the delusion that the physical, created world is able to satisfy the longing of our heart. In some way you and I are always spending our money in the search for satisfaction of some kind. The reality of forever confronts the "If only I had _____, then I would be happy" paradigm that shapes so much of what we do with our money.

Surely one of the purposes of the physical world is to give you enjoyment, but it will never be your savior. You simply cannot find horizontally the life that every human being searches for. All the glories of this physical world are designed to point you to the existence of a God of awesome glory, who alone is able to satisfy your heart. The satisfying glory of eternity is not about location. No, it's about him. Sin will no longer separate us from him. Creation will no longer compete with him for our worship. We will be with him in heart-satisfying communion forever.

So the truth of the eternity to come protects me and my

money from that devious lie, first told in the garden, that life can be found outside of relationship to the Lord of life. I am convinced that so much of our selfish and unwise spending is an attempt to buy life, to buy the satisfaction that we reason has so far eluded us. Eternity reminds us every day that we cannot buy with our money what only grace can provide. In so doing it protects us from craving what we do not need in the hope that it will provide what it cannot give. *Are you spending money in the hope that you can buy what money will never provide?*

4) The existence of eternity tells me what I should be investing my resources in. It tells me what will bring me the greatest return.

In two statements of stunning wisdom, Jesus summarizes how eternity is meant to shape what you invest in. He said, "Do not lay up for yourselves treasures on earth" (Matt. 6:19); and "Pray then like this: . . . Your kingdom come, your will be done, on earth as it is in heaven" (Matt. 6:9). Two short pieces of messianic brilliance that capture what it looks like to invest your money with eternity in view. Don't allow the principal purpose of the investment of your funds to be the amassing of earthbound treasures. Don't expend your resources on things that will quickly break, grow old, get stolen, decay, or otherwise pass away. But we do let the warehousing of physical stuff drive our spending, so much so that many of us have to rent storage space because our houses, as big as they are, are not big enough to hold the piles of physical stuff that we have used our money to accumulate.

The Lord's Prayer captures the flipside of Jesus' investment wisdom. Consider the request that comes first and is meant to shape everything else you ask God for. "Your kingdom come, your will be done" is a comfort and a call. You have been welcomed by God into a kingdom that is much greater, much more beautiful, and much more heart satisfying than whatever kingdom you could work to construct for yourself. And you have been called to submit your life and resources to the work of a kingdom bigger than your own.

Grace has freed me from my bondage to me and in doing so has enabled me to invest in things bigger than me. Grace has freed me from my bondage to making short-term investments in things that end up complicating life and indebting me. Grace allows me to be excited with the eternal significance of the work of God's kingdom. Grace changes my heart and focuses my eyes. Grace helps me to weep over a lost and dying world. Grace helps me to long that others would know the peace of heart that I have come to know. Grace causes me to loosen my tight-fisted grip and offer what does not belong to me for the greater purposes of the One to whom it does belong.

Now, it's not wrong to spend your money on physical life necessities. It's not wrong to invest in your health care and retirement. But it is wrong if that is all you do. Remember, the prayer "Give us this day our daily bread" is only ever to be prayed in the context of the first and greater request, "Your kingdom come." *Do you joyfully invest in things of eternal significance?*

5) The existence of eternity clarifies my values
by alerting me to what is truly important.

We all have a values problem. Here it is: this side of eternity it is very hard to value in our heart what God says is important. Things tend to rise in levels of importance way beyond their true importance and command the attention, allegiance, and investment of our heart. It's not wrong to want a comfortable life, but comfort must not rule our heart. It's not wrong to desire beautiful surroundings, but the physical beauty of the place we live must not rule our heart. This is where Christ's word "treasure" is helpful. Few of the treasures that become important to us have intrinsic value. That's what is behind the old saying, "One man's trash is another man's treasure." We are constantly assigning value to things, and once we have worked to gain those things, we work to maintain, enjoy, and protect them. So whether we know it or not, we always spend our money in pursuit of what we consider valuable. In our everyday life, to the degree that we value what God says is valuable, to that degree we will spend our money wisely.

Here's where the reality of eternity can help us. In his Word God invites us to eavesdrop on eternity. We get to listen to the words of saints who have finished their journey and are on the other side. As they look back on their lives from eternity, we get to hear what is valuable to them and, in listening, have our values clarified. The saints on the other side don't look back with thankful hearts and say, "We wore the best clothes," or "We lived in the finest houses," or "We amassed the greatest wealth." Rather, from the perspective of eternity, the things that seem so valuable to us don't hold much value to them. What they celebrate is redemption—that God defeated every enemy, made good on every promise, and did exactly all he said it would do.

I recognize that I still have a values war raging in my heart and that, at times, values confusion shapes my spending. So I still need to hear the voices from the other side to remind me of what is truly important in life. I still need to be rescued from investing heavily in things of little eternal value while I neglect what is truly important. *Does your spending depict that you need to have eternity correct your values?*

6) The existence of eternity tells me the danger of giving way to the temptation to worship the creation and not the Creator.

I have written so much about this that I won't write much more here. But I can't resist reminding you that this is the question of questions. Your use of your money is an act of worship. Your spending depicts a worship of the Creator, the creation, or a troubling mix of both. You and I never spend money neutrally. We always worship our way through our bank accounts. And often our use of money reveals that at some level we have exchanged worship and service of the Creator for worship and service of his creation. Remember, worship is not just something we do in formal church gatherings. No, you and I worship our way through every moment of every day. So it really is impossible that our use of money not be an act of worship. Eternity reminds us that God alone is worthy of the moment-by-moment worship investments that will shape and direct our life. It is right to spend money in the enjoyment of the creation, but only in a way that worships the One who made it. *What does your spending reveal about who or what commands the worship of your heart?*

7) The existence of eternity assures me of the grace I need to fight the money battles that will wage in my heart.

If you and I are guaranteed a place with our Lord in eternity, then we are also guaranteed all grace we will need along the way. Let me put it this way: the future grace of eternity carries with it the promise of present grace. You see, if God's grace can't keep us in the here and now, how could he ever promise the eternity that is the bright hope of redemption? So eternity reminds us that between the already and the not yet, there are no spiritual battles that we will fight in our own strength.

What does his grace provide me with right here, right now? The answer is him! He is the greatest gift of his grace. My weaknesses are so great and my need so profound that the only thing that can help me is him. So he unzips me and gets inside by his Spirit. What does this mean for me and my money? It means that I never face money temptations by myself. I never have to fight money battles with the small resources of my own strength. And he works not only to deliver me from the temptations of a world that has gone money mad but from something much more dangerous: my own wandering heart. He delivers me from me, by progressively transforming my heart. He causes me to think in new ways, to desire new and better things. He lovingly corrects my values. He gives me the grace to say no and the power to flee. And he fights money battles on my behalf even when I don't have the sense to. This means my hope is more secure than that I will just get money matters right. My hope is in this one thing: that he has invaded my life by his grace and will not stop forgiving, transforming, and empowering me until these things are no longer needed. And he will not lose me to money or to anything else. *Do you forget who you are and give way to money temptations that grace empowers you to fight?*

8) The existence of eternity gives me hope when I get sex and money completely wrong. I hope not in my track record but in his.

This side of eternity you and I will get money wrong again and again. This side of eternity we will have moments when we listen to the lie and try to buy with our money what money cannot buy. This side of eternity there will be times when we will worship what is not worthy of our worship and forget the One who is. This side of eternity we will go through times when we are poor stewards of the resources that God has entrusted to us. When it comes to money, we won't perfectly measure up. At best, we will all have a spotty track record.

This is exactly why God offers us his grace. He went to the extent that he did to send and sacrifice his Son because there was no other hope for us. Even with our knowledge of and submission to his law, we continue to mess up. Even in the face of elaborate theological understanding, we wander away. Even with knowledge of his presence and promises, there are times when we're disloyal. Grace has freed us from cataloging our righteousness and commending our track record to him. And grace has freed us from running from him when we are aware that we have nothing of ourselves to commend. Grace frees us from both money self-righteousness and money despair. There is no money mess so deep that his grace isn't deeper. We don't spend in the hope of earning his love. No, our spending is being transformed by his love. And when we mess up again, we know that his love will simply not let us go.

Here is the bottom line, and it's important to remember it when you're fighting money battles in your heart: no human hero is celebrated in eternity. God is celebrated. All the humans are there by means of his rescue. *Do you give way to the dangers of money self-righteousness* (thinking you've defeated your last money enemy) *or of money despair* (thinking that when it comes to money there's no hope for you)?

As you try to deal responsibly with money in the middle of a world that has gone money insane, just remember every time you put your hand on your wallet to focus your eyes on eternity, celebrating its comfort and surrendering your funds to its call.

14

ARE YOU LIVING LIKE YOU'RE POOR?

The missionary told a compelling story, one that got my attention and still has it today. He was ministering in a horribly impoverished country to people who literally had nothing. One time as he was walking to the market to get provisions, he happened across a wandering pack of little boys. He didn't have much money himself, but his heart went out to these boys, who have little hope and a dark future ahead of them. He reached into his pocket and gave the boy who seemed to be the leader of the pack the equivalent of ten American dollars. That boy held riches in his hand that he had never imagined and would surely never see again. "Use it wisely," the missionary said as he went on his way.

After purchasing his provisions, the missionary walked home from the market along the same road. He heard the sounds of happy chatter before he saw the same pack of little boys. To his shock and surprise each of the boys had ice cream in his hand. The missionary couldn't believe what he was seeing. Immediately anger well up inside of him and he took the leader of the pack aside and scolded him, saying, "I gave you more money than you've ever seen, and this is what you do with it?" With little hesitation the boy responded, "Sir, yesterday we were poor, tomorrow we will be poor, but today we have ice cream."

You see, poverty is not just a condition; it becomes an identity. What the boy was saying is, "You do get it, mister. I am poor; I will always be poor. Your money won't keep me from being poor, so today I'll numb myself with pleasure, because I have no hope of anything ever changing." Sadly, many people who call themselves Christians and say they believe in the gospel of the Lord Jesus Christ live with a poverty mentality. They feel that they have nothing to face what they daily need to face; they have little hope of ever having anything, so they numb themselves with the pleasures of the moment. But there is something underneath the poverty mentality.

I am convinced that there is much confusion of identity in the body of Christ. I am convinced that there are many believers who simply don't know who they are. Now, this is a very significant thing, because every rational human being assigns some kind of identity to him- or herself. In that influential and informative self-conversation we are always having, we tell ourselves who we are. And the identity we assign to ourselves then determines how we go about dealing with the stuff on our plate.

When you have *confusion of identity*, you will tend to live with a *poverty mentality*, which makes you a sitting duck for *sex-and-money insanity*. It is only riches that can deliver you from riches. What do I mean by this? It is only the heart-satisfying riches of the grace of Jesus that can protect and free you from the deceptive and dissatisfying "riches" of this fallen world. Only when your heart is content can you have lasting protection against becoming addicted to the temporarily satisfying pleasures of the created world. It is vital to understand the riches that you have been given in Christ. It's essential to approach life as one who is rich. It makes no sense to go out on the street and beg when you have been given an inheritance beyond your wildest dreams.

• • •

He sat slumped in the chair with his head down once again. He had the look of an utterly defeated and hopeless man. He had come to see me, but he didn't want to be there, and he had said a few things, but he had no interest in talking. No trial had brought him to this point. No, he had finally seen himself with accuracy, and what he saw had taken his breath away. He now knew that his struggles were bigger than he had ever imagined and his weakness much greater than he had assessed. After what seemed to be hours of silence but was actually less than a minute, he looked up at me and said, "I don't think I've ever felt more weak and discouraged." The moment he said it, I was relieved. He was right—his story was a chronicle of weakness. He was right—there was no hope for him all by himself.

If you can stare your personal sex-and-money insanity in the face and say, "No problem, I can handle this," you are a person in deep, deep spiritual trouble. It is only when you are crushed by your poverty of desire, ability, and hope that you begin to get excited about the riches that are yours in the grace of the Lord Jesus Christ. And it is only when you daily read to yourself the gospel of those riches that you will have the insight and courage to fight the battles that God calls and graces you to fight.

I knew in that moment that I would not help him by minimizing the daily temptations he was facing. I knew it wouldn't help him to negate the power of the war he was living in. I knew it wouldn't help him to pump up his assessment of his own strength. To do any of those things would have been to play into the deceptive power and attraction of sex-and-money insanity. As I sat there with him, I was once again reminded that hopelessness is the doorway to hope. It's only when we abandon our hope in our own righteousness, wisdom, and strength, and it is only when we abandon our hope that the created world will be our savior that we will then reach out for the riches of the righteousness, wisdom, and strength found only ever in Jesus.

Who do you tell yourself that you are? Do you assign to yourself riches of independent righteousness and strength that you don't have? Do you assess that you are wiser than you really are?

Or do you preach to yourself of your aloneness, poverty, and inability? Are you better skilled at convincing yourself that you are more hopeless than a person of robust hope? You see, both the "I can handle this" believer and the "There is no hope for someone like me" believer suffer from the same thing: *identity amnesia*. They have been saved by the blood of Jesus, but between their past forgiveness and their future in eternity, they have simply forgotten or never truly grasped who they are. So they will not seek the help they need, rest in the grace they've been given, or fight their battles with the weapons they've been given by grace.

RICH GRACE

It is one of my favorite passages of Scripture. It has been a longtime friend. It gets me up in the morning. It reminds me who I am, it helps me to correctly assess what I have been given, and it gives me courage to face the battles of the day. It is one of those passages in which God paints a beautiful word picture for us:

> Come, everyone who thirsts,
>   come to the waters;
> and he who has no money,
>   come, buy and eat!
> Come, buy wine and milk
>   without money and without price.
> Why do you spend your money for that which is not bread,
>   and your labor for that which does not satisfy?
> Listen diligently to me, and eat what is good,
>   and delight yourselves in rich food.
> Incline your ear, and come to me;
>   hear, that your soul may live;
> and I will make with you an everlasting covenant,
>   my steadfast, sure love for David. (Isa. 55:1–3)

What a gorgeous picture of the heart-satisfying pleasures of grace! You will never understand who you are, what you have been given, and the resources that are yours right here, right now until you understand that as God's child you have been invited to dine at the banquet table of the King. It is an invitation you couldn't have bought. It is a meal you don't deserve. Yours is food you couldn't have earned. It's only when you get who you are and the table that grace has put your feet under that you will quit trying to feed your soul on what will never satisfy it. It's only resting in the riches that you have been given that will free you from seeking riches where they cannot be found. Only a full and satisfied heart is free from the insanity of a ravenous heart. It's only when you are eating with joy the food of the King that you quit seeking food elsewhere. It's only when you rest in the reality that you have been given life that you quit looking to money and sex to give you life. It's when you begin to understand that you've been invited to a meal that will never end, that you've been welcomed to the King's table forever, that you'll quit looking to sneak a bite at other tables.

THE RICH FOOD OF REDEMPTION

So what does it actually look like to affirm your identity as a child of God and live in light of his lavish resources of grace? What does it mean to approach the struggles of sex and money from the perspective of the gospel of Jesus Christ? What new ways of living would result from your living as if you really did believe that you have been welcomed to the soul-satisfying banquet table of the King of kings? What is the right-here, right-now gospel that each of us must preach to ourselves every day to protect ourselves from the sex-and-money insanity that is often inside us and everywhere around us? Below is a starting place.

1) I am never alone.

In your struggle for God-honoring stewardship and purity, you must tell yourself again and again that if you're God's child, if you have been redeemed by his grace, and if you have been welcomed into his eternal family, it is absolutely impossible for you to ever be alone. There is no situation, no relationship, no location, and no struggle in which you exist all by yourself. No, your life has been invaded by the Savior, the King, the Lamb, the Captain, the victor Jesus Christ. He is your spiritual life. He is your power, your wisdom, and your hope. He is the food and the drink at the King's table. God's most wonderful gift to us is not a thing; it is a person. Our need was so great, our battle with sin so profound, that he knew the only thing that would help us was himself. So he gave us himself in the gift of his crucified, resurrected, and indwelling Son.

This means I can no longer look at my life and my struggles with sex and money in a "me against the world" way. I cannot allow myself to assess my potential to defeat the next temptation based on my previous track record and the size of the thing I am facing. I can't go around thinking that I've been left to my ingenuity and strength. This kind of thinking denies the gospel realities of who I am and what I have been given. The presence of the Lord with me always belies any personal assessments of aloneness or inability.

Now, this reality of his presence is counterintuitive for us. Doubt, fear, anxiety, envying another's life, wondering if you have what it takes, and wishing life were easier is natural; but living in light of the constant presence of the Redeemer isn't. This is why it is so important to preach this truth to yourself again and again.

2) I have all the resources I need.

The apostle Paul says that God has "blessed us in Christ with every spiritual blessing" (Eph. 1:3). He also ends his discussion of life in the fallen world in Romans 8 with these words: "He who did not spare his own Son but gave him up for us all, how will he not also with him graciously give us all things?" (v. 32). Peter writes to suffering and struggling people these encouraging words: "His divine power has granted to us all things that pertain to life and godliness" (2 Pet. 1:3). Yes, God has chosen to keep us for a time in this fallen world where the full range of the temptations of sex-

and-money insanity exist and in some way greet us every day. Yes, we still live in a world where the Devil lurks about as a ravenous beast. And it is true that between the already and the not yet we still carry around inside of us the susceptibility to sin. But it is not true that we have been left on our own without any resources.

Grace means that God will not leave you on your own and he will never call you to a situation or location without giving you what you need to do what he has called you to do. So I must at times flee, and there are times when I must stand and resist. I must avoid the tendency to name myself as more wise, righteous, and stronger than I actually am. I must resist the dark lie of the enemy that comes to me in a variety of forms and is seeking to get me to believe that life can be found outside of the Savior. I must fight the draw to look for heart satisfaction in things like sexual pleasure and money power. I must deal with my temptation to love the creation more than I do the Creator. I must always watch what I surrender my heart to. But I do none of these things in my own power or with my own resources. I can stand and affirm that I have no power on my own to either resist or defeat sin and be perfectly at rest, because I have been blessed with the rich resources of amazing grace. I don't have to hope that I'll have what I need. No, the cross assures me that I already have in my personal spiritual storehouse everything that I could ever need. Could it be possible to preach this to yourself too much?

3) I am forgiven.

What often drives the sex-and-money struggle underground, giving it room for sin to do its ugly work, is the powerful triad of self-righteousness, guilt, and shame. First, in an act of irrationality I attach my inner sense of well-being to my own righteousness, forgetting that the best of my righteousness is like a filthy rag, so I try to prove to God and myself and demonstrate to others that I am righteous. Because of this, I minimize, deny, excuse, rationalize, or shift the blame for my sin. I work to make myself feel good about what is not good. I recast my own history, and I rewrite my own stories, all for the purpose of self-atonement. Meanwhile the insanity of sex-and/or-money addiction is growing in my heart.

Or I panic in the face of the clear sex-and-money evidence that I am not righteous at all. I give way to fear because I blow it in big and small ways again and again. And in moments when I am not acting out, I am constantly attracted to or desiring things that I should not. I cannot escape the guilt of my street-level unfaithfulness and am not able make it all look okay. So I hide in shame, fearing the rejection of others and the anger of God. I cannot believe that God could place his love on a person like me. This too is a function of debilitating self-righteousness that completely forgets the gospel of Jesus Christ.

It doesn't matter how exotically righteous you are. It doesn't matter how pure you are in your dealings with sex and money. It doesn't matter how strong you are against temptation. Your standing with God is never based on your righteousness, but on his. His perfect life, his acceptable death, and his death-defeating resurrection guaranteed your standing with God. All of your sins past, present, and future have been covered by his blood. His righteousness has been attributed to your account. So even in your moment of greatest failure, you do not have to hide from God or fear his presence. Your penalty has been paid and eternal acceptance has been granted, so you can run into God's presence, lost and broken as you often are, without fear of his rejection. Grace guarantees your forgiveness, pays the penalty for your guilt, and lifts the burden of shame off your shoulders. You simply can't preach forgiveness to yourself enough.

4) There is someone who understands me.

The writer of Hebrews assures us with these words: "We do not have a high priest who is unable to sympathize with our weaknesses, but one who in every respect has been tempted as we are, yet without sin" (Heb. 4:15). In writing these words, the author exposes one of the cruel lies of the enemy. This lie is meant to paralyze you as you seek to battle the temptations of sex and money. The lie goes this way: "No one understands what you're going through because no one is dealing with what you're dealing with." This lie is not only fashioned to get you to embrace the discouraging thought that no one could ever understand you because you are utterly alone in your experience, but it is also designed to do something even more debilitating. It is designed to get you to doubt the goodness of God. Here is the underbelly of this lie: "No one will understand you, because you have been singled out. Look around you; no one is going through what you've been going through. Maybe God has forgotten you. Maybe he is not always there. Perhaps he does, in fact, have favorites. Maybe he doesn't always answer prayer." All this is meant to get you to doubt God's goodness, because if you don't trust his character in your moments of sex-and-money temptation, you won't run to him for help.

But the writer of Hebrews says that the exact opposite is true. In a grace-driven desire that you have just the right help in your moment of sex-and-money need, Jesus exposed himself to every kind of temptation you face so that you would always know that you seek help from one who knows exactly what you're going through. And because he knows exactly what you're going through, he is able to offer you help that is form-fit for you and for the battle of the moment. So you don't have to give way to the hesitation of doubt. No, you can go to him with complete confidence. He knows, he understands, and he greets you with the sympathy of someone who has not only been there but has defeated what you now need to defeat. Wow! There is not a day when you and I don't need to hear this.

5) Change is possible for me.

All this means that no matter now many times I have failed, how many times I have said yes to what required a no, or how defeated

I feel, I am not stuck; change really is possible. My existence has been taken over and altered by powerful zealous and unstoppable grace. No matter how great my sin, no matter how foolish I am, and no matter how messy my track record, grace will ultimately win. God's kingdom will come. His will will be done. He will not relent until every microbe of sin is delivered from every cell of every heart of every one of his children.

In our battle with sex-and-money insanity, you and I are blessed to be the sons and daughters of a zealous and dissatisfied Redeemer. He doesn't get discouraged. He doesn't panic when things are hard. He doesn't wonder if he made the wrong choice in placing his grace on you. He doesn't wring his hands and wish the problem would go away. He won't give up with the job half done. And he surely won't drop his work in you and walk away. You can change, not because you have the right motives or the right amount of power, but because he will not sit down until the final enemy has been defeated.

You and I simply cannot allow ourselves to give way to the paralysis of hopelessness. Yes, there will be moments when change does look impossible. There will be times when it seems that things are getting worse, not better. There will be times when we will be tempted to wonder if God is there and if he is who he has declared himself to be. There will be times when we'll wonder if grace has forgotten our address. But we must remember that our Redeemer is not like us. He would never, ever consider forsaking the work of his hands. He is covenant-ally committed to completing in us what he has begun. Our hope for change rests not so much on our character, but on his. Now, that's good news!

6) Weakness is not my big problem, but my delusion of strength is.

Here are paradigm-changing words, words that are designed to revolutionize what you think about yourself and life in this fallen world: "My grace is sufficient for you, for my power is made perfect in weakness" (2 Cor. 12:9). When you think you're strong, or when you work to make yourself believe you're strong, you won't seek and rest in the powerful grace you have been given in Christ Jesus. We all just need to get a grip. Our stories present ample evidence that we are, in fact, quite weak, and in our weakness, quite susceptible to surrendering to things we should resist. We have all given way to sex-and-money temptations that we should have run from. But we needn't panic. God knows just how weak we are. He is not shocked or surprised by the evidence of our lack of power. No, his grace isn't thwarted by our weakness. The opposite is true: his grace does its best work precisely at the moment when our weaknesses have been exposed.

You see, our hope rests not in the size of our strength but in the inestimable magnitude of his. Grace can deal with all of our weaknesses, but when we tell ourselves that we're strong, we have little interest in that grace. It would do all of us a whole lot of good to listen to the message that our struggle with sex and money preaches. There are few areas in our lives that preach a gospel of neediness more than our struggles with sex and money. If you listen to that message, you will be a seeker and celebrator of the powerful grace that has been lavished on you.

7) I have been given rich wisdom for daily living.

One of the sad effects of sin is that it shrinks all of us to fools. We don't need any more evidence of the foolishness of sin in the stupid choices human beings make than what we do with sex and money. Consider King David's adultery with Bathsheba. What was he thinking? In his mind, what was the end game? What did he imagine God would do? Did he really think he would get away with it? How did he convince himself that this illicit relationship was okay and would end okay? What a powerful picture of the foolishness of sin. Or what about Christ's story of the rich young man who would rather retain his wealth than have a relationship with the Messiah himself? Was he really so foolish as to think he could have the best of both worlds? Did he actually have no understanding of what really ruled his heart? Did he really think that turning his back on Jesus was the better choice?

Foolishness is the problem of every human being because it is one of the inescapable effects of sin, and we are all sinners. We cannot escape this foolishness, because we cannot escape ourselves. So it is here that the gospel of Jesus Christ greets us with such power. The gospel declares that wisdom is not first a book, a blog post and tweet, or a theological essay. No, wisdom is first a person, and his name is Jesus. Paul says in Colossians 2:3 that Jesus is the one "in whom are hidden all the treasures of wisdom and knowledge." To rescue us from our foolishness, God gave us the only thing that would help—his Son.

But not only have we been given the Son, who is the Word, also we have been blessed with the Word of the Son. Every page of Scripture gives us wisdom that we do not have on our own. There are things you need to know as you struggle with the sex-and-money insanity that lurks inside you and all around you, things you would never know by means of personal experience and collective research. These vital truths are known only by means of revelation.

So God gifts us with his Word so that we may know him and his plan, so that we may understand ourselves and our needs, and so that we may know where lasting hope and help can be found. The purpose of God's Word is not so much to give us religious and theological information but for our personal transformation. So the Son, who is the Word, and the Word of the Son mean that we are not left to our own foolishness. There is one who is wisdom, who gifts us with wisdom we would never, ever have without him. We need to tell this to ourselves again and again.

8) It is only the riches of grace that satisfy my heart.

I don't need to say much more about this, other than repeat that this is a truth we need to preach to ourselves every day. You and I will only ever get vertically the heart satisfaction we all seek. It simply cannot and will not be found horizontally. Every created thing is without the capacity to satisfy your heart. The created world was designed to point you to where your heart will find its contentment and rest: in God and God alone. The sex-and-money insanity that harms and/or destroys our lives is the result of seeking from creation what can only be found at the foot of the Creator.

9) It's guaranteed that my struggle with sex and money will end.

The victory of Jesus assures your victory. In farming terms, he is the first fruits. The appearance of the first apple on the tree is a guarantee of more apples to come. The empty cross and tomb of Jesus is your guarantee that the sex-and-money sin in your life will someday be defeated and you will live forever and be free of its internal and external insanity. That guarantee of its future defeat is also a guarantee of all the grace you need along the way.

Yes, we do live in a world that has gone sex-and-money insane. And, yes, that insanity still lives in some way in all of our hearts. But we needn't panic; we needn't succumb; we needn't think that our battles are leading nowhere. We must not give way to assessments of poverty, aloneness, and impossibility, because the insanity has been invaded by the Messiah, Jesus. He faced every insane thing we face, and he defeated it all on our behalf. He did all this so that you and I would have the grace we need to face the sex-and-money struggles that we will continue to face until eternity is our home and the insanity has been quieted forever.

GENERAL INDEX

Adam and Eve, 31, 56; God's boundaries for, 60–61; hiding from God, 137; nature of, 57–58. *See also* fall, the; garden of Eden

addiction, 22–23, 65, 133, 177

aloneness, 138–40

"already" and the "not yet," the, 78, 79, 80, 88

antinomianism, 87

anxiety, 187

asceticism, 57; misunderstanding of the nature of God's creation, 57; misunderstanding of the nature of human beings, 57–58

authority, 113–14

autonomy, 115, 153

big-picture sex, 71–74, 81–82; as connected to God's eternity, 80; as connected to God's existence, 74–75; as connected to God's glory, 75–76; as connected to God's purpose, 76–77; as connected to God's redemption, 78–80; as connected to God's revelation, 77–78

body, the, as God's temple, 93–94, 123

boundaries, 60–61, 117–19

church, the: as community, 138–39; the evangelical church's lack of honesty, integrity, and biblical accuracy, 51–52; silence of regarding sex and money, 17

compassion, 183

confession: to God, 52–54, 94, 106, 123, 125; relational confession, 109

contentment, 173–75, 183

creation, 30–31, 75, 115. *See also* creation, implications of for our use of sex and money

creation, implications of for our use of sex and money: because we are created in God's image, all of life is spiritual,

33–34; God exists and is the center of all things, 28–30; God is the creator and owner of all that exists, 30–32; the purpose of the cross is to reconcile us to God, 38–39; since God is the creator of all things, he alone is worthy of our worship, 34–36; when it comes to sex and money, we have bought into the spiritual versus secular dichotomy, 36–37

desire, 48; loading of into our need category, 147; ruling desire, 48, 61, 66, 178

destination mentality, 192

discontent, 148, 168–69, 173–75

disobedience, 121–22; and the claim to greater wisdom, 121; and the claim to ownership, 121–22; and self-swindling, 79, 122

doubt, 187

Eden hermeneutic, 56, 63

entitlement, 173, 177–78

envy, 148, 168

eternity, 80, 185, 186, 189. *See also* eternity, implications of for our use of money; eternity, worship principle of

eternity, implications of for our use of money, 190–91; eternity clarifies our values when it comes to spending, 195–96; grace empowers us to fight money temptations, 197–98; grace frees us from both money self-righteousness and money despair, 198–99; our money has a bigger purpose, 191–92; our use of money is an act of worship, 196–97; our use of money should be shaped by a preparation mentality, 192–93; we cannot buy with money what only grace can provide, 193–94; we must joyfully

215

invest in things of eternal significance, 194–95

eternity, worship principle of, 86, 90–91, 94

eternity amnesia, 90, 185, 187–88, 190

fall, the, 58, 62, 188, 189

fallen world, the, 18, 80, 135–37, 151, 175, 189–90, 206–7

fear, 137–38, 187

foolishness, 211–12

garden of Eden, 31, 56, 61; nature of, 57

glory, 23–24; the glory battle, 24; pleasure as God-glorifying, 58–60; self-glory, 174, 175, 179; sign glory, 24; ultimate glory (the glory of God), 24, 29, 58–60, 75–76, 193

God: as the center of all things, 28–30; as the creator and controller of all things, 34–36; as the creator and owner of all that exists, 30–32; existence of, 74–75; glory of, 24, 29, 58–60, 75–76, 193; goodness of, 149; love of, 140; purpose of, 76–77; as a spirit, 33–34. *See also* grace; redemption; revelation

gospel, the, 19, 21, 89. *See also* gospel, the, implications of for our use of sex; grace

gospel, the, implications of for our use of sex, 131–32; we can live in a new and better way, 141–42; we can quit thinking that change is impossible, 141; we don't have to be ashamed that we are sexual beings, 132–34; we don't have to deny that we are sinners, 134–35; we don't have to deny the fallenness of the world around us, 135–37; we don't have to fight our battles alone, 138–40; we don't have to hide in guilt and fear, 137–38; we don't have to question God's patient love, 140

grace, 38–39, 49, 74, 92–93, 96–97, 123, 134, 138, 142, 149, 156, 169, 181–82, 182–83, 195, 198, 207, 208, 209, 210, 211, 212–13; assurance of, 197–98; the celebration of pleasure with the celebration of grace, 65–66; and our misplaced treasure hunting ("playing with the box"), 165–67; richness of, 204–5. *See also* redemption, implications of for our use of sex and money

gratitude, 147, 183

guilt, 66, 137–38, 207, 208

heart, the, 25, 28, 58, 79, 147; and behavior, 48–49, 51–52; as the causal center of personhood, 47–48; as a control center, 48; as deceptive, 50–51; the eyes of the heart, 159–60; as fickle, 50, 88, 168, 169, 180; Jesus' teachings on, 44–47, 48–49; money as a window on what rules our hearts, 150–51; as susceptible, 49–50; and willingness, 116–17; as a worship center, 48

hermeneutics, 56

hiding, in guilt and fear, 137–38

honesty, 134

hope, 89, 93, 105, 140, 198, 211

"I am a danger to myself" lifestyle, 176–77, 180–82; "I deserve," unquestioned, 177–78; "I want," unrestrained, 178; "I will," unchallenged, 179–80; "me first," undebated, 179

identity, 175, 202; confusion of, 202

identity amnesia, 204

image of God, 33–34

ingratitude, 147

insanity (cultural), 13–17, 20–23, 73, 202, 213; and buying into the spiritual versus secular dichotomy, 36–37; and the evangelical church's lack of honesty, integrity, and biblical accuracy, 51–52; money insanity, 15–16, 17–18, 32, 186, 187–88, 191–92, 193; sexual insanity, 13–15, 16–17, 32, 83–84, 97, 111, 113–14, 116, 119, 134

Jesus, 181; his teachings on the heart, 44–47, 48–49; his teachings on investment, 194–95; his teachings on the kingdom of God, 167–78; his teachings on money, 143, 146, 160–64, 194–95; his teachings on treasure, 46, 159, 160–62, 188, 194, 195; as the true treasure, 167–69; as wisdom, 212; as the Word, 212

kingdom of God, 152, 155, 168, 194–95; Jesus's teachings on, 167–68

Lord's Prayer, 179, 194–95

love, 102; God's love, 140

mastery, worship principle of, 86, 87–89, 94

me-ism, 29–30, 73, 97. *See also* practical me-istic presentism (PMP) money, 143–49; the blessing-danger battle of money, 143–45; as the creation of God, 18; as deeply spiritual, 34; and discontent, 148; and envy, 148; as the expression of the spirituality of life, 34; and God's grace, 182–83; and ingratitude, 147; insanity of, 15–16, 17–18, 32, 186, 187–88, 191–92, 193; Jesus's teachings on money, 143, 146, 160–61, 162–64, 194–95; money despair, 199; money self-righteousness, 199; and need, 147; as a significant theme throughout Scripture, 143–45; use of money as an act of worship, 155. *See also* money, as a blessing; money, as a dangerous thing; money, and eternity; money, love of; treasure hunting

money, as a blessing: as a means of responding to the needs of others, 151–52; as a way to connect us to the work of the bigger kingdom, 152; as a window on the dangers of the fallen world, 151; as a window on the goodness of God, 149; as a window on what rules our hearts, 150–51

money, as a dangerous thing: money can cause us to forget God, 152–53; money can cause us to look down on others, 154; money can change the way we think about ourselves, 153–54; money can finance our allegiance to the kingdom of self, 155–56; money can weaken our resolve to fight temptation, 154–55

money, and eternity. *See* eternity, implications of for our use of money; practical me-istic presentism (PMP)

money, love of, 147; as a contentment problem, 173, 173–75; as a fallen world problem, 173, 175; the four ingredients that set up our hearts to love money (ingratitude, need, discontent, envy), 147–49; as an identity problem, 173, 175; as the root of evil, 172–76; as a worship problem, 173, 176. *See also* "I am a danger to myself" lifestyle

need, 147

obedience, 35–36, 116–20, 123; "without challenge," 119; "without delay," 119–20; "without excuse," 119

ownership, worship principle of, 86, 93–94, 94

ownership living, 32

parenting, and the discussion of sex and money with children, 17–18, 37

patience, 183

pleasure: asceticism's misunderstanding of, 57–58; the celebration of pleasure with the celebration of grace, 65–66; as God-glorifying, 58–60; and God's boundaries, 60–61; as God's creation, 56–57; the pleasure of God, 61–62; as seductive and deceptive, 62–63; what are we are asking of our pleasures? 63–65

pornography, 21, 107, 109–10

poverty mentality, 201–2

practical me-istic presentism (PMP), 186; PMP acts as if this moment is all there is, 186–88; PMP hopes that paradise is achievable now, 189–90; PMP thinks that material things can satisfy, 188–89

preparation mentality, 192–93

reconciliation: to God, 25, 38–39; relational reconciliation, 109

redemption, 78–80, 196. *See also* redemption, implications of for our use of sex and money

redemption, implications of for our use of sex and money: change is possible for us, 209–10; it is guaranteed that our struggles with sex and money will end, 213; it is only the riches of grace that satisfy our hearts, 212–13; there is someone who understands us, 208–9; we are forgiven, 207–8; we are never alone, 205–6; we have all the resources we need, 206–7; we have been given rich wisdom for daily living, 211–12; weakness is not our big problem, but our delusion of strength is, 210–11

relationship: with God, 32, 33–34; and sex (*see* sex, and relationship)

revelation: general revelation, 27; special revelation, 27 (*see also* Scripture, as God's special revelation)

Scripture, 196, 212; boundary view of, 86–87; deep, personal agenda of, 191; as God's special revelation, 27, 77–78

self-love trinity (my wants, my needs, my feelings), 174

self-righteousness, 207–8

self-sufficiency, 115, 153

self-swindling, 79, 122

service, 36, 183, 197

sex: in advertising, 107; as the creation of God, 18; as deeply spiritual, 34; individualization of, 83–84, 85, 116; insanity of, 13–15, 16–17, 32, 83–84, 97, 111, 113–14, 116, 119, 134; little-picture sex, 71–74, 80–81, 82; sexual dysfunction and married couples, 108–9; sexual purity, 103, 105, 117, 122–25. *See also* big-picture sex; gospel, the, implications of for our use of sex; sex, and obedience; sex, and relationship; sex, and worship

sex, and obedience, 113–16; sex and disobedience, 121–22; and sexual purity, 122–25; what obedience looks like, 116–20

sex, and relationship: sex as inescapably relational (a living commitment to community), 100–101; sex and loving God, 101–6; sex and loving our neighbor, 106–11

sex, and worship, 84–87, 123; and the worship command to flee sexual immorality, 95–96; and the worship command to glorify God in our bodies, 96–97; and the worship principle of eternity, 86, 90–91, 94; and the worship principle of mastery, 86, 87–89, 94; and the worship principle of ownership, 86, 93–94, 97; and the worship principle of unity, 87, 91–93, 97

sexuality, as God's gift, 132–34

shame, 207, 208

Sibbes, Richard, 132–33

sin, 49, 79, 105, 134–35; sexual sin, 47, 101, 102, 106–7, 132–35

sober celebrant, 93

spiritual schizophrenia, 33, 180–81

spiritual versus secular dichotomy, 28, 33, 36–37

treasure hunting, 159–65; Jesus's teachings on treasure, 46, 159, 160–62, 188, 194, 195; our misplaced treasure hunting ("playing with the box"), 165–67; and the true treasure (Jesus and his grace), 167–69; what a treasure is, 46

Tripp, Tedd, 116

trust, 36

unity, worship principle of, 86, 91–93, 94

values, clarification of, 195–96

worship, 34–35, 60, 196–97; as bowing down, 35; as obeying, 35–36; as serving, 36; as trusting, 36; worship of the creation, 176. *See also* sex, and worship

SCRIPTURE INDEX

Genesis
1:1   27–28, 38
3   58, 137

Exodus
3:12   139

Deuteronomy
15:10   144

Joshua
1:5, 9   139

Judges
6:12   139

2 Samuel
7:9   139

Psalms
51   53–54
62:10   133

Proverbs
3:9–10   145
10:15   144
16:8   144
22:7   145
23:4   144
28:20   144

Ecclesiastes
3:11   186
5:10   144

Isaiah
55:1–3   204

Hosea
4:11   133

Malachi
3:10   145

Matthew
5:27–30   44–45
6:9   194
6:19   46, 194
6:19–33   159
6:24   160–61
6:33   163
13:44–46   167–68
19:21   163
24:17   133
28:20   139

Mark
7:20–23   46

Luke
6:24   163
12:15   163
12:20–21   163
12:32–33   163
12:34   144
16:10–11   145
18:24–25   163–64
21:43   133

John
14:15   102

Acts
20:25b   145

Romans
1   135, 175
8:18–39   136–37
8:32   206
12:1   123

1 Corinthians

6:12–13	87
6:12–20	85
6:13a	88
6:14	90
6:15	91, 92
6:19–20	93

2 Corinthians

5:15	111
5:20	25
12:9	210–11

Ephesians

1:3	206
4:16	139

Colossians

2:3	212

1 Timothy

6:6–10	172–73
6:9	144
6:10–11	143

Hebrews

4:15	208–9
13:5	139, 144

James

1:17	149
4:1–3	145

2 Peter

1:3	206

CENTER FOR

PAST🔥RAL
LIFE AND CARE

"As pastors we must confess our daily need for everything we teach and preach to others."
~ Paul Tripp, *Executive Director*

ABC
ASSOCIATION *of* BIBLICAL COUNSELORS

www.pastorlifeandcare.com | (855) 319-2752

A DVD teaching companion to
Sex and Money